Spelling Anything

Spelling Anything

...Even Pneumonoultramicroscopic-silicovolcanoconiosis

A Guide to Becoming Your Regional
Spelling Bee Champion and Qualifying for
the Scripps National Spelling Bee

AKASH VUKOTI

WASHINGTON, DC

Copyright © 2025 by Akash Vukoti

The usage of the terms "Scripps National Spelling Bee," "Scripps," "National Spelling Bee," and "Nationals" in this book does not imply any endorsement by the Scripps National Spelling Bee or the E. W. Scripps Company.

All rights reserved. No part of this book may be reproduced, stored, or transmitted by any means—whether auditory, graphic, mechanical, or electronic—without written permission of both publisher and author, except in the case of brief excerpts used in critical articles and reviews. Unauthorized reproduction of any part of this work is illegal and is punishable by law.

Vicara Books | www.vicarabooks.com
All trademarks are the property of their respective companies.
Cover Design by Vanessa Mendozzi
Interior Design by Zoe Norvell

Cataloging-in-Publication Data is on file with the Library of Congress.
ISBN: 978-1-64687-189-6

Special Sales
Vicara books are available at a special discount for bulk purchases for sales promotions and premiums, or for use in corporate training programs. Special editions, including personalized covers, a custom foreword, corporate imprints, and bonus content, are also available.

1 2 3 4 5 6 7 8 9 10

I dedicate this book to the Supreme Lord, whose guidance and blessings have been my constant source of strength and inspiration.

I express my deepest gratitude to my family—my parents (Chandrakala and Dr. Krishna Vukoti) and my wonderful sister (Amrita)—for their unwavering love and support.

Most importantly, I wish to thank my amazing followers around the globe—over 1 million plus across YouTube, Facebook, and Instagram—whose encouragement has been the biggest motivation for writing this book!

Acknowledgments

I extend my heartfelt thanks to the four awesome champions listed below for taking the time to review this book and provide valuable, constructive feedback!

KERRY CLOSE
2006 Scripps National Spelling Bee Champion
(A special thank you for judging the TV show *Harry's Spelling Bee* competition between me and Harry Connick Jr. in 2017!)

DEV SHAH
2023 Scripps National Spelling Bee Champion

BRUHAT SOMA
2024 Scripps National Spelling Bee Champion

YASH SHELAR
Placed 23rd in the 2022 Scripps National Spelling Bee

Contents

1. Introduction...................................1

2. Why the Spelling Bee?...............5

3. Insights into the Spelling Bee.................11

4. Preparation for the Spelling Bee............25

5. Language Rules...................41

6. Root Directory...................121

7. Vocabulary Tips...................133

8. Strategies for Spelling Words Onstage...141

9. After the Bee...................161

CHAPTER 1

Introduction

PNEUMONOULTRAMICROSCOPIC-SILICOVOLCANOCONIOSIS! THIS IS A 45-LETTER-LONG behemoth and one of the longest words in the dictionary today. You may have seen me spell this long word in Hollywood next to Steve Harvey (as seen using the following QR code), on *Dancing with the Stars*, on TV, or on social media. YES... I'm Akash Vukoti! At six years old in 2016, I became the youngest boy to compete in the Scripps National Spelling Bee. With a record of six appearances at the national level, I am the most experienced speller at the regional level. Many people have reached out to me via my YouTube channel, website, and other social media platforms, seeking advice on how to prepare for and

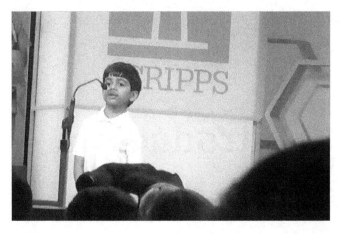

Competing on stage at the 2016 Scripps National Spelling Bee when I was 6

excel in the spelling bee. While I've responded to as many as possible, I realized I could compile all my knowledge into a book. My goal is to share the 11 years of experience I've gained from competing in spelling bees with you. This book aims to equip you with the tools you need to win your regional spelling bee and qualify for the Nationals!

You might be reading this because you're a student attracted by the intriguing cover of this book, or perhaps you're a parent who dreams of watching your child shine on that D.C. stage. You may have seen the Bee on live television or social media and envisioned yourself spelling words at the world's most prestigious academic competition. No matter who you are, if your aim is to excel in your regional competition and secure a spot at the Scripps National Spelling Bee in D.C., this book is perfect for you! I've written this for ordinary students passionate about spelling who aspire to become extraordinary by qualifying for the elite Scripps National Spelling Bee. If you're not sure where to start, this book will serve as the starting point for the long journey toward the national stage.

Each year, a select group of around 250 spellers qualify to the Nationals from an initial pool of about 11 million students worldwide. Making it to the National Bee may seem like a daunting challenge, but not to worry; in this book, I have provided a wealth of valuable tips, tricks, and strategies to help you excel in your local bees and join the ranks of those elite spellers. The book explores language rules and spelling patterns that form a strong foundation, root words that are crucial for mastering the dictionary, and effective strategies for correctly spelling your words onstage.

This book is designed not only to improve your spelling abilities but also to teach you the techniques that top spellers use to thrive, both while preparing and onstage. If you follow this book and work hard, you'll be well-equipped to tackle even the toughest challenges at the regional level, and ultimately, earn your spot at the National Spelling Bee. I assure you, the sense of accomplishment in becoming one of the top spellers in the world is unmatched, and it offers a significant confidence boost that will highly benefit you later in life.

The journey toward earning your spot at the National Spelling Bee starts here—each page brings you one step closer to success!

CHAPTER 2

Why the Spelling Bee?

THE SPELLING BEE IS MORE than just a competition—it's a celebration of the English language, memory, and the skill to spell the words correctly. For over 100 years, the spelling bee has established itself as a hallmark of American culture. Below are some of the benefits of competing in spelling bees.

Increasing Vocabulary and Knowledge

The spelling bee challenges you to not only spell difficult words but also to understand their meanings, origins, and correct usage. By studying for the bee, you'll expand your lexicon and gain valuable insights into word structure, etymology, and pronunciation. This fosters a deeper connection to language, making it a great tool for

Playing in the "alphabet soup," a pit of foam blocks at the 2019 Scripps National Spelling Bee

enhancing vocabulary. You'll be looking at words from a whole new perspective for the rest of your life!

In addition, delving into the world of words offers a wealth of knowledge. As you prepare for the spelling bee, you also gain valuable insights into etymology, the origins and histories of words, improving your overall knowledge. For example, more than a third of the words in the English dictionary are French-derived. This is because the French ruled over England during the 11th and 12th centuries. This is a fact that you would learn because of all the French words you studied while preparing for the spelling bee. Furthermore, because of the wide range of English vocabulary, you'll acquire foundational knowledge across every subject, which will greatly benefit you in college. For example, if you opt to study biology, you'll already have a familiarity with the terminology used in that field thanks to the biology words you encountered during your spelling bee preparation.

Love of Learning

Beyond the immediate goal of winning, the spelling bee instills a deep appreciation for the process of learning. It inspires students like you to engage with language in a fun, interactive way and promotes the idea that learning should be a lifelong pursuit. The bee is not only a competitive event but an invitation to explore the rich, diverse world of English words and their meanings. This spark of curiosity is contagious, motivating children to take an active interest in language, literature, and education in general. For many children, the spelling bee marks the beginning of a passion that goes well beyond the competition. Once you have the passion for spelling, it's for life!

Cognitive Benefits

Spelling requires a unique combination of cognitive skills. You need to integrate your memory, attention to detail, and problem-solving abilities as you recall language patterns and apply your knowledge of rules like prefixes, suffixes, and phonetics. The mental challenge of spelling difficult words under time constraints sharpens concentration and enhances memory retention. These cognitive abilities go beyond just spelling bees; they play a significant role in enhancing academic performance in school and will positively impact future professional endeavors.

Competitive Spirit

Just as football is a physical sport, the spelling bee is a mental sport, and both incorporate a competitive spirit. The spelling bee fosters this by emphasizing individual accountability and clear goals. Contestants are driven by the need to perform well in a high-pressure environment, where each correctly spelled word brings them closer to victory. The merit-based competition encourages participants to push themselves to excel. The drive and determination to win will take you very far in life, even beyond spelling bees.

Building Confidence to Speak

There is a clear difference between spelling a word at your home, and spelling a word on stage with a time limit and an audience watching you. The spelling bee gives every speller the opportunity to stand in front of the audience, and offers a chance to overcome nerves.

As you spell out words before an audience, you're

building confidence in your abilities to perform under pressure. The spelling bee experience can be empowering, boosting self-esteem and enhancing communication skills—all assets that will allow you to achieve incredible things in your life. The self-assurance that you gain from competing at the bee will have a lasting impact, helping you feel more confident when you are called upon to speak or present ideas in front of others.

Dealing with Adversity

Participating in a spelling bee fosters resilience by demonstrating how to navigate adversity. The pressure of speaking before an audience and tackling challenging words create an environment where failure is a genuine possibility. You're not going to win every spelling bee you compete in; that is practically impossible. The spelling bee encourages you to persevere, learn from your mistakes, and enhance your skills. The competitive nature of the event pushes you to stay focused, manage stress, and bounce back stronger after setbacks, which fosters mental strength and the ability to face challenges with determination. The spelling bee serves as a reminder that it's perfectly fine to lose or for others to be ahead of you; what truly counts is the effort you invest and the lessons you take away from the experience.

Making Friends

When you're competing onstage, it's not you against someone else; you're competing against the half a million words in the dictionary. Although the joy of learning and the pride that comes from mastering something challenging are important, the friendships formed during this event are truly special. Whether you advance to the final round or not, the spelling bee creates a supportive community where your fellow students share the same passion as you. Ultimately, the spelling bee is a wonderful opportunity to build friendships that will last for a lifetime.

In conclusion, the spelling bee is far more than just a contest of spelling prowess. It is a versatile event that promotes the enhancement of English vocabulary, strengthens cognitive abilities, fosters public speaking skills, and builds self-confidence. It celebrates hard work, perseverance, and a love of learning, while providing a platform for young people like you to shine. As a 100-year-old tradition, the spelling bee continues to inspire generations, demonstrating the significance of language and the lasting importance of education.

CHAPTER 3

Insights into
the Spelling Bee

FOR ALMOST 100 YEARS, THE National Spelling Bee has been held annually during the week of Memorial Day, bringing together the world's top spellers in Washington D.C., the nation's capital. The National Spelling Bee actually starts from a pool of over *11 million schoolchildren* from the US and around the world. Competitors participate in several local bees, including class, school, region, and even state spelling bees (Alabama, Arkansas, Connecticut, Georgia, Hawaii, Maine, Mississippi, Montana, Nevada, New Hampshire, New Mexico, North Dakota, Rhode Island, South Dakota, Vermont, Wisconsin, and Wyoming are the states that, to my knowledge, organized a state bee in 2024). There are also around 10 other countries and territories that compete in the Scripps National Spelling Bee, including the Bahamas, Canada, parts of Europe, Ghana, Guam, Jamaica, Japan, Puerto Rico, South Korea, and the U.S. Virgin Islands. I anticipate that a few other countries will join the Scripps National Spelling Bee in the coming years. From all of these competitions, only around 250 top spellers earn a spot at the National Spelling Bee in Washington D.C. Securing your spot at the Nationals is a tough challenge, so let's dive into the details of the spelling bee format and the steps you need to take to reach the national stage!

Note: All of the information in this section is accurate as of the time I am writing this; for up-to-date information, please check the Scripps National Spelling Bee website at spellingbee.com.

Eligibility, Rules, and Regulations

I would like to emphasize a few important points from the official rules of the National Spelling Bee.

The most crucial factor is eligibility, as it dictates whether you can participate. The general eligibility criteria is as follows: a) participants must be in eighth grade or lower, b) they must be 14 years old or younger, c) they should not have previously won the Scripps National Spelling Bee, and d) they cannot repeat a grade solely to remain eligible for competition. If you satisfy these conditions, you are likely all set to compete.

All of the words that will be asked at the National Spelling Bee come from *Webster's Third New International Dictionary, Unabridged*, which is available online at unabridged.merriam-webster.com with a subscription. If you become a regional spelling bee champion and qualify for the Nationals, you are awarded a free coupon for a one-year online subscription to *Merriam-Webster Unabridged*. This online version of the dictionary has the Advanced Search tool, which is extremely helpful in finding words with specific patterns and features. Stay away from other dictionaries, because they may have words and other information that is not in *Merriam-Webster Unabridged*.

When it is your turn, you have a total of 90 seconds once the pronouncer gives you your word to ask questions and spell it. This means you have a limited amount of time to get as much information and clarification as you can before you spell your word. Furthermore, if you begin spelling a word and ask to restart midway, you may do so as long as you maintain the order of the letters you have already spelled.

Since 2021, the National Spelling Bee has introduced vocabulary (word meaning) rounds into the competition, in which you will have 30 seconds to answer a multiple-choice question about the meaning of the given word. This means you will need to dedicate time to not only learn the spellings but also understand the meanings of each word. Learning the meanings of words significantly enhances your overall knowledge, and it can even help you remember the spellings of many words.

These are a few important guidelines; for comprehensive information regarding eligibility, rules, and regulations, I strongly suggest visiting the Scripps National Spelling Bee's website or reaching out to their official team. Now that you're familiar with how the National Spelling Bee operates, you can anticipate your local competitions to follow a similar format. In some cases, they may even be more restrictive. When I was first starting out as a five-year-old, there were quite a few local bees with a minimum age or grade limit, and that meant I couldn't compete in them. Nevertheless, be sure to check with your local bee organizer for additional details, as they may have different procedures (details on how to do this are in the following pages). Now, let's take a look at the local bees to learn how you can make it to the National Spelling Bee.

Journey to Nationals

The path to the National Spelling Bee starts in the classroom, where spellers progress through several local competitions before making it to Washington, D.C. Depending on your location, the types of local bees may vary. For example, I advanced through my class, school, and regional bees before qualifying for the national competition. Additionally, some spellers are required to take part in district or county bees, while several states also hold their own state bees in addition to these other levels. There are even national contests for countries beyond the United States that take part in the National Spelling Bee. You likely have a different set of local bees to compete in within your area before you can qualify for the Nationals. I highly encourage you to check what local bees you will be competing in. You can find this information by asking your teachers, talking with friends who have participated in local bees before, or searching using your ZIP code on the Scripps National Spelling Bee website to reach out to the local bee coordinator. At the time of printing this book, the ZIP code search option is available on the enrollment page of the website (spellingbee.com/enroll).

What to Do If Your School Doesn't Have a Spelling Bee

The first step toward the National Spelling Bee is to make sure that your school is enrolled in the national competition in the first place. You can check this by using the ZIP code feature in the enrollment page linked on the previous page. If your school is enrolled, ask your teachers about the classroom and school spelling bees, and also for the *Words of the Champions* word list (more information in the following pages). If your school is not enrolled, then either you or your parents can discuss the idea of enrolling the school into the Bee with your English teacher, school principal, or another school official. I recommend doing this in October or November, a month or two before the usual time for classroom- and school-level bees.

If you are homeschooled, as I was during my time in the Spelling Bee, you can participate by joining a local homeschool association in your area. A great way to begin is by asking your parents about options available. If there are no associations nearby, you can still register your homeschool individually through the Spelling Bee's enrollment page. This is a simple overview of what I did to compete at Scripps; the National Spelling Bee's FAQ page has more detailed information.

What to Do If Your Region Doesn't Have a Spelling Bee

If you reside in an area without a regional spelling bee, you might be wondering how to make it to the National Spelling Bee. Here are a few steps you can take to make that happen: First, try reaching out to regional bee organizers from previous years, if available. Their experience running the regional bee can be invaluable in reviving the spelling bee program in your area. If you can't contact previous organizers, consider reaching out directly to the National Spelling Bee for guidance on organizing a regional bee. It's a good idea to reach out to sponsors—often media outlets, universities, or businesses—to fund your regional bee, as most local competitions rely on sponsorship. If you can't find sponsors, the National Spelling Bee can facilitate an at-large regional competition, which they have organized in the past for schools that registered but did not have a regional spelling bee.

Word List for Local Spelling Bees

Preparing for spelling bees can seem overwhelming at first, as it might feel like spellers have to memorize all half a million words in the dictionary. However, most local competitions actually rely on the recommended 4,000-word study list from the Scripps National Spelling Bee, called *Words of the Champions*. The words in this list change every year, and the National Spelling Bee releases the new list at the beginning of each academic year, before the spelling bee season begins. *Words of the Champions* contains 4,000 words that you MUST master to qualify for the Nationals, since almost every word used in local spelling bees will come from this list. In fact, as of the time of writing, *Words of the Champions* serves as the source for the initial spelling and vocabulary rounds of the National Spelling Bee. If you are committed to competing at the national level, it's crucial to learn both the spellings and meanings of every word on the list. *Words of the Champions* is organized into different difficulty levels: One Bee (beginner), Two Bee (intermediate), and Three Bee (advanced). Each of these difficulty levels includes a School List (for classroom and school bees) as well as the actual *Words of the Champions* list (for regional contests and the initial rounds of the Nationals). If your regional bee includes a vocabulary component, you should learn not just the spellings, but also the meanings of the words in this list.

Consider reaching out to your family, friends, or teachers to assist you in mastering these words by quizzing you or reviewing them together. Furthermore, the Scripps National Spelling Bee offers an app called "Word Club," allowing you to test your knowledge on the *Words of the Champions* whenever you like, right from your phone or tablet.

Now, let's explore the various stages of competition leading up to the National Spelling Bee, along with several important details you should be aware of before participating.

Class Bee

The class spelling bee usually marks the beginning of your journey to Scripps. In this competition, you'll face off against fellow students from your grade at your school. Most class bees utilize the School List in *Words of the Champions*; however, this may vary based on your local competition, so make sure to check with your teachers. The words shouldn't be very difficult, and as long as you familiarize yourself with the word list, you should perform well at the class level. Class bees typically take place in December or early January, so make sure to ask your teachers about it ahead of time. In some schools, there may not be a class bee, and the competition then proceeds directly to the school bee, so it's important to know which format your school is implementing. If you win your class bee, you will advance to the school spelling bee.

School Bee

The school spelling bee typically occurs after the class bee, where you'll compete against the champions from each class within your school. These contests generally cover the School List, and may also include some words from the main *Words of the Champions* list. If you've prepared for the more challenging words, you should find this bee quite easy to handle. The school bee is usually held in mid- to late January. Your teachers and the spelling bee coordinator can provide valuable information about both the class and school spelling bees. If you win your school bee, you'll advance to the next level of competition, where you'll face off against other school champions from around your region.

Regional Bee

Typically, school champions advance straight to their regional spelling bee. Many organizers host a single regional spelling bee after the school-level competition. However, in some larger regions, an additional district spelling bee may take place before the regional bee. For example, the Dallas Regional Spelling Bee has district spelling bees leading up to the main regional competition. Furthermore, around 17 U.S. states organized state spelling bees after the regional level in 2024, and there have been about 10 other countries and territories around the world that organized nationwide spelling bees to send a competitor to Scripps.

The number of spellers competing in your regional spelling bee can vary significantly based on your location and the competitiveness of your region, ranging from 25 to well over 100 participants. These events typically take place in late February and continue throughout most of March.

It is common for all competitions after the school spelling bee to use the entire *Words of the Champions* list as the primary source. However, if the competition is particularly fierce, the organizers may choose words that are not in the official list and come directly from *Merriam-Webster Unabridged* dictionary; these words are called "off-list words." In some regional bees, organizers might start with a written preliminary test containing spelling and/or vocabulary questions, only allowing those who score above a certain cutoff to advance to the oral rounds. That's why it's very important to familiarize yourself with the meanings of the words in *Words of the Champions*. I highly recommend contacting your regional spelling bee coordinator for more information. In the next chapter, I will provide some effective strategies for spelling bee preparation that you can use to excel in your regional bees.

Me and my family after I won the 2016 San Angelo Regional Spelling Bee and qualified for the first time to the Scripps National Spelling Bee

National Spelling Bee

Once you win your regional spelling bee, along with the awards you may receive, your regional bee coordinator will provide information about how you can register for the National Spelling Bee. They will usually hand you an envelope containing an ID and password to log in and register for the Nationals. This is where you can upload your photo, fill in all of your details, and submit signed release forms for the Bee.

The National Spelling Bee takes place throughout the week of Memorial Day, the last week of May, at the Gaylord National Resort & Convention Center in

National Harbor, Oxon Hill, MD, near Washington, D.C. Registration takes place on Sunday and Monday, when most spellers arrive, and as it is the National Capital Area, the Bee organizes trips to National Museums or parks on Monday. The Preliminaries begin on Tuesday, with the Quarterfinals and Semifinals on Wednesday, and the Finals taking place on Thursday evening. The Bee Bash, an awards banquet and farewell party, takes place around Friday evening, and most people leave either on Saturday or Sunday.

All words used in the National Spelling Bee come from *Merriam-Webster Unabridged* dictionary, and the first spelling and vocabulary rounds of the Preliminaries specifically use *Words of the Champions* as the source. Each phase of the competition (Preliminaries, Quarterfinals, Semifinals, Finals) has one vocabulary round in addition to the spelling rounds. In 2021, the National Spelling Bee introduced a tie-breaking Spell-off, which is triggered if the Finals last almost 2 hours. In that case, the last remaining competitors have to correctly spell as many words as possible in 90 seconds.

Bee Week has definitely been one of the most memorable weeks of my life, and I'm sure that it would be the same for you!

My sister, my dad, and me during a fun outdoor activity at the 2016 Scripps National Spelling Bee

A caricature artist drawing a picture of me during the 2016 Scripps National Spelling Bee

CHAPTER 4

Preparation for the Spelling Bee

THE MOST DIFFICULT PART OF the spelling bee is that there is NO room for error; one mistake and you'll hear the dreaded bell sound, signaling that you'll have to wait a whole year for another shot at the National Spelling Bee. This highlights the importance of meticulous preparation to achieve success in the spelling bee! Let's explore some of the preparation strategies that helped me succeed at the class, school, and regional levels.

Finding Word Lists

The first step towards the Scripps National Spelling Bee is figuring out what words you should learn at the regional level. That's why it's so important to start by finding the right word lists to study. The official regional bee word list, *Words of the Champions*, is the most crucial, as it serves as the foundation for nearly all local bees, beginning with the class bee. It is absolutely necessary for you to master both the spellings and the meanings of every word in *Words of the Champions*. If you're looking for off-list words that regional spelling bee organizers might ask, there are a few lists to consider studying: 1) Previous editions of *Words of the Champions*; 2) *Spell-It!*, the National Spelling Bee's old regional study guide; 3) the *Consolidated Word List*, an old word list that the National Spelling Bee published; and 4) *Paideia*, an older study guide used prior to *Spell-It!*. All of these resources can be easily found on the Internet. Furthermore, there are plenty of apps and online tools that you can use to study word lists. Word Club, the National Spelling Bee's official platform for learning *Words of the Champions*, is the main app you should consider using. You can also use Quizlet for flashcards or Vocabulary.com for vocabulary quizzes, among many other options. Some paid platforms, like SpellPundit, offer complete word lists for spelling and vocabulary practice. Finding and mastering word lists is the most effective way to prepare for spelling bees.

Writing Your Own Word Lists

The most enjoyable aspect of my preparation for the spelling bee was creating my own word lists. It's an excellent method to familiarize yourself with new vocabulary. You can organize these lists by themes, such as words related to biology, law, engineering, music, or any other subject. You might also group words by their origins, like French, German, or geographical terms. Another effective strategy is to focus on spelling patterns; for example, you could compile all words that start with a silent *p* or just nouns that end in *-ous*. You can also make lists of homonyms, words that are pronounced identically, or compile words with surprising or confusing pronunciations.

The two key lists I made consisted of the most challenging words to remember: the "Big List" and the "Small List." I made it a point to review both of these lists every weekend. I added every difficult word that I studied into the "Big List." Whenever I encountered a word from the "Big List" that was exceptionally challenging, I would move it to the "Small List." These are lists you build over time, and by familiarizing yourself with the words as you practice, you can curate the lists and minimize the number of entries. By the time I was in eighth grade, the "Big List" included approximately 10,000 words, and the "Small List" featured around

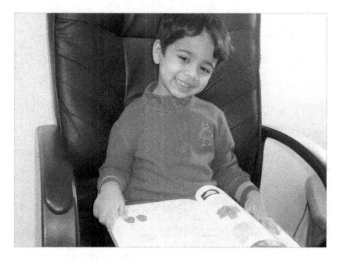

Three-year-old me reading my favorite book: the *Merriam-Webster's Primary Dictionary*

3,000 of the most difficult words from the 500,000 words in the dictionary. In the week leading up to the Bee, I dedicated all my study time to the "Big List," and then concentrated specifically on the "Small List" the day before. A spreadsheet program like Excel is a great tool to create these lists, as it is very simple and easily searchable.

If you subscribe to *Merriam-Webster Unabridged* online, you can utilize the Advanced Search feature to categorize words based on spelling, definition, language of origin, part of speech, and even subject. You can search for words with specific prefixes and suffixes by adding an asterisk before or after the search term. For example, to locate words that begin with *ps-*, simply

enter "ps*," and for those that end with -*ette*, type "*ette."
These are some of the most effective techniques for
compiling new word lists.

When it comes to creating word lists, I suggest
consolidating all your lists in one place. By keeping
everything organized by category or difficulty, you make
it easy to find the specific list you want to review at any
given time. As your local bees approach, you may want
to focus on more challenging words, and staying organized helps you locate those lists effortlessly. Moreover,
this method can spark new list ideas by highlighting
gaps you may have overlooked. For instance, if you have
lists for words beginning with "*gn-*" and "*pn-*," it could
inspire you to create a list for words starting with "*kn-*"
and so forth.

Study Every Day

When I competed in the spelling bee, the most important habit I had was to study consistently every day.
Regardless of my daily activities, I always made time
to sit down and learn new words. The amount of time
you spend studying for the spelling bee can vary, but
I recommend studying for a minimum of one hour a day
on weekdays and significantly longer on the weekends.
This study time can differ depending on the time of year.
I typically ramp up my preparation as the spelling bee

draws nearer, often increasing my study sessions to several hours a day. At times, you may not be able to spend as much time studying words, but you should always try to compensate for that on the weekends or whenever you can. Adjust your specific focus based on the upcoming spelling bee. If the school bee is approaching, concentrate on the School List section of *Words of the Champions*; if the regional bee is next, shift your attention to the entire *Words of the Champions* list; and if you happen to qualify for the National Spelling Bee, get ready to tackle the entire dictionary.

I have a deep passion for language, and English holds a special place in my heart. When you are passionate about something, the motivation to learn more automatically comes with it. I am sure you are very passionate about spelling, and so I am very confident that you can find time to study.

Review Consistently

An important step in getting ready for spelling bees is to consistently review words. Remembering words is just like remembering people: You might easily recognize the U.S. president at a glance, but you may struggle to remember every person you've ever seen. The more frequently you see someone, the easier it becomes to remember them, and the same applies for words. This is why consistently revisiting the words you've learned is so important. You can do this by creating lists and practicing them every so often, writing challenging words on Post-it Notes and placing them around your room, or having someone you know quiz you on those words. I suggest you take time to review whenever possible: while waiting for your ride, on the bus, in between classes, or even on your phone. There are countless creative ways to reinforce your memory of difficult words, so choose what works best for you.

Ask for Help

When it comes to learning new words, your family, friends, and teachers can be your greatest allies! Be sure to get their help as much as possible. You can ask them to quiz you on word lists, help you create lists, review *Words of the Champions* and other study guides with you, or even practice spelling patterns together. I always worked together with my family. My mom prepared word lists for me to study, my dad quizzed me daily, and my sister and I would review words together all the time. While being quizzed, try to simulate the experience of an actual spelling bee. By replicating the actual competition format, you can boost your confidence and deal with nervousness. There are plenty of fun activities that you can do with those around you—trust me, it will all pay off when you compete in the bee!

My big sister, Amrita, quizzing me as part of my preparation for the Regional Spelling Bee

Me and my sister as toddlers, reading the words in the *Merriam-Webster's Primary Dictionary*

Fix Mistakes

One crucial aspect that I used to improve my performance at the spelling bee was fixing my mistakes. Whenever I misspelled a word in quizzing, I learned where I went wrong, and then figured out how I could prevent that mistake from happening again. Usually, that means making lists of words relating to trick spots, getting accustomed to new spelling rules, or in some cases, plain memorization. If you get used to doing this during preparation, it can reinforce your knowledge of the toughest words in the dictionary, making you ready to handle off-list words.

Check the "Word of the Day"

Many online platforms offer "Word of the Day" services, which are excellent tools for expanding your vocabulary. Merriam-Webster has a "Word of the Day" series that you can subscribe to via email, and the Scripps National Spelling Bee shares a "Word of the Week" on their Facebook page every Wednesday. Since 2019, I've been hosting a "Word of the Day" series on my YouTube channel. You can scan the QR code to check it out, and subscribing to my channel will ensure these videos appear in your Recommended page. Other resources like Dictionary.com,

Oxford English Dictionary, and *Cambridge Dictionary* have their own "Word of the Day." However, be cautious when using these alternate dictionaries, as they may include words that are not listed in *Merriam-Webster Unabridged*, which is the official dictionary for the spelling bee.

Look for Good Words

If you encounter an interesting word that you're unfamiliar with, make it a practice to write it down and explore its meaning—this is a great method to enhance your performance in spelling bees. One excellent resource for discovering new words is the newspaper, where articles often showcase a diverse and rich vocabulary. For example, the New York Times website has sections dedicated to spelling and vocabulary quizzes, providing a fun and interactive way to broaden your lexicon. To further enrich your word bank, consider utilizing vocabulary-building apps that present you with new words each day. Incorporating these words into your daily conversations or writing will reinforce your understanding and help you remember their spellings and meanings. Incorporate newly learned words in your daily conversations to develop a deeper grasp of how they are used. Consistency and curiosity are crucial—by continuously challenging yourself, you'll gradually improve both your spelling and vocabulary skills in range and depth.

Review Words from Previous Years

Words that appeared in the Semifinals or Finals of previous National Spelling Bees sometimes show up in the first few rounds of newer bees. For instance, the word *drahthaar* was asked in the finals of the 2016 National Spelling Bee and later reappeared in *Words of the Champions* 2024. It even got asked in Round 1 of the 2024 Nationals! Search for previous years' National word lists on the Internet and note down the words that you find challenging or intriguing, as they may show up in *Words of the Champions* or potentially even as off-list words.

Search for Newly Added Words to the Dictionary

Merriam-Webster introduces several hundred new words to the dictionary at least once a year and shares these on their free blog, Wordplay (merriam-webster.com/wordplay). You can easily find this information by searching for "Merriam-Webster newly added words," which will lead you to links for each word along with some interesting facts. Although these newly added words may not appear in most spelling preparation lists, bee organizers can still ask them in competitions. This is the best way to discover these words so you won't overlook them in your preparation.

Memorize Words Using Mnemonics

Memorizing the spellings of the most challenging words in the dictionary can be tricky. However, it's often easier to remember a rhyming phrase instead, much like how we all can recall song lyrics. These rhyming phrases are a type of mnemonic, which is a sentence that helps you remember something. For instance, the phrase "i before e except after c" is a well-known mnemonic that encapsulates a general English spelling rule. If you can find similar mini-rhymes or other mnemonics, it becomes much easier to remember words that might otherwise be very difficult to spell correctly.

Compete at Practice Spelling Bees

All of the above topics that we have discussed will definitely better prepare you for the spelling bees, but practice makes perfect, right? Some spelling bees are not affiliated with the Scripps National Spelling Bee, and are just practice bees that you can compete in to test your skills and see where you stand in the field of competition. I competed in many of these bees over my spelling bee career, and I urge you to compete in these practice spelling bees before you compete at the actual Scripps Regional Spelling Bee—it's the best form of practice for your regional bee.

One issue with most practice spelling bee events,

especially more recent ones, is that they don't last very long (i.e., they are held for a few years, and then never again). There is one big exception to this: North South Foundation (NSF), has successfully held spelling bees and other academic events nationwide for over 25 years and established themselves as the largest player in the practice spelling bee field. North South Foundation was founded in 1989 by Dr. Ratnam Chitturi as a nonprofit to help economically disadvantaged children in India get the education they need, and they fund this by organizing academic competitions, like spelling bees, in the United States. I competed at NSF for 11 years from 2013 to 2023, and it is a great way to prepare yourself for regional bees, as well as the Nationals. NSF has multiple regional chapters around the United States, which organize spelling bees for their respective areas. The spelling bee is divided into two parts: Junior Spelling Bee (JSB) for 1st, 2nd, and 3rd grades, and Senior Spelling Bee (SSB) for 4th grade and above. The top placers in JSB and SSB from each regional chapter qualify for the NSF National Finals, held in a different university campus every single year. The regional and national bees each have their own word list to study. Most of the words that will be asked are taken from this list, just like *Words of the Champions* for the real regional bee. The spelling bee consists of two phases: Phase I, which is a 25-question written test (10 words are from the study list), and Phase II, which is a 6-round oral spelling bee with no elimination (all 6 words are from the study list). The National format has a few changes, the most notable being a final Phase III, which works like the real spelling bee finals: competitors get eliminated whenever they misspell a word, and the winner is the last speller standing. I recommend NSF as a great starting point for practice spelling bee competitions.

Me after securing third place at the NSF National Finals in 2018—matching my finish from the previous year in 2017

The next one on this list is the SpellPundit National Online Spelling Bee. This bee was started in 2020 by SpellPundit, a company offering spelling and vocabulary word lists to practice, and it works in a very similar fashion to the real National Spelling Bee. It, too, is divided into Junior and Senior subsections, and the word choice is of a national level, especially in the final rounds, so I recommend you join if you are serious about becoming the regional spelling bee champion and doing well at the real National Spelling Bee.

The same goes with Scott Remer's Words of Wisdom Online Spelling Bee, also founded in 2020, and aimed at the top echelon of competitors. Scott Remer has written valuable resources for National Spelling Bee preparation, and his Words of Wisdom Bee is another great way to practice for the regionals and Nationals.

There may be other practice bees just like these ones, but many of them only happen occasionally or depend on funding to continue.

When you register for these practice spelling bees, they usually give you a study list to start with, like NSF. It's crucial to study these words and know them thoroughly, because aside from the practice bee itself, these words are very likely to be the type of words that your regional bee, and maybe even Nationals, will ask. Ultimately, it's becoming familiar with as many words as possible that is the key to the championship, and competing in as many practice bees as possible is the best way to see where you place amongst the crowd and prepare for the real deal.

Search for Words from Other Regional Bees

Search online for the words that have been asked at previous regional spelling bees. If your regional spelling bee is scheduled later in the season, you'll have an added advantage since there will be more spelling bees to review. It is likely that the words you see in those competitions will also appear in your regional bees, especially the off-list words. Make sure to keep an eye on local news outlets for updates regarding regional spelling bees; you might discover not only the winning word but also a comprehensive list of all the words that were asked. Additionally, some regions broadcast their spelling bees live on YouTube or Facebook, and some cities even air it on TV, such as Houston, TX (Houston Public Media Spelling Bee), and Norfolk, VA (WHRO Spelling Bee).

Have Fun

You're reading this book because you have a passion for spelling and the English language; it won't feel like you're working hard if you're enjoying the process. Having fun was the most important part of my entire spelling bee experience. If you're not enjoying it, then it's not worth your time. I continued preparing for the spelling bee throughout all of my eligible years, regardless of the outcome, because of my passion for the English language and words. I thoroughly enjoyed this phase of my life, and I hope you find it just as exciting as I did!

CHAPTER 5

Language Rules

NOW THAT WE'VE EXPLORED ALL the essential tips for your spelling bees, it's time to dive into the fascinating realm of language-specific spelling patterns! English has a rich history of borrowing words from various languages, and since we seldom alter their spellings, the origin of a word plays a significant role in how that word is spelled. Each language has its own set of spelling patterns or rules for how to spell each sound; by learning these rules, you will master the majority of words in the English language, because they all follow these patterns. This section of the book focuses on every major language you can expect to see at your local bees and all the important rules to know when you're spelling words from those languages.

I've organized these languages based on how frequently they tend to appear in spelling bees, with those at the top being much more common than those toward the bottom. However, it's essential to learn all the rules, as you never know what kind of word might come up during the competition. I also strongly recommend looking up each example word in this chapter using *Merriam-Webster Unabridged*. Not only are these excellent spelling bee words, but they also serve as starting points for deeper exploration, helping you create valuable word lists and discover even more great words to study.

Note: It is standard practice to use the Merriam-Webster pronunciation diacritics system (a guide to the system is in the QR code below) to notate how words are pronounced.

OLD ENGLISH and MIDDLE ENGLISH

Old and Middle English are the early stages of the English language, spoken in Great Britain from around 500 AD to 1470. They were shaped by significant historical influences from Old Norse, French, and Latin. Old English has contributed much of English's core vocabulary, and Middle English supplemented it with loanwords from French and Latin that were modified to fit native English spelling rules. Since then, English has consistently adopted words from a variety of languages around the globe due to the British Empire's colonial influence, continually expanding its vocabulary even to this day.

Due to recent Anglicization, words from Old and Middle English are spelled very similarly to words in Modern English, but there are still a few key features you might want to focus on. Listed below are the important patterns in these languages:

Vowels

» The schwa \ə\, also known as the "uh" sound, can be spelled with nearly every vowel (*anent, heretoga, chariot, gersum*), and even *eo* (*luncheon, sconcheon*) and *ou* (*dyvour*).

» The dotted schwa \ə̇\ sounds like an unstressed "ih" sound, and it can be spelled *e, i,* or *ei* (*mullein* is one example of this) in Old and Middle English.

» \ä\ is usually *a* (*balm*) or *o* (*obley*).
» \ā\ is generally either *a* or *ai* at the start or middle of words (*acre*, *wainscot*), and *-ay* or *-eigh* at the end of words (*allay*, *counterweigh*).
» \ē\ is usually *-y*, *-ie*, or *-ey* at the end of words (*dreary*, *tydie*, *hackney*), and *i*, *e*, *ee*, *ea*, *ei*, or *ie* (*finial*, *prepense*, *leeward*, *feasible*, *ceiling*, *siege*) in the middle. Middle English is the origin of the *-ly* adverb ending, so whenever you see \-lē\ at the end of a word, spell it *-ly*. The *-ie* ending is commonly found in words that have some relation to Scotland, so if you hear "Middle English" AND "Scots" in the language of origin, consider spelling the \ē\ ending *-ie*.
» \i\ is mostly spelled *i* (*hayrick*), with a few cases of *ei*, like *weir*.
» \ȯ\ can be spelled *o* (*alembroth*) or *au* (*hauberk*).
» \ō\ at the end of Old English words is *-ow*, which might seem odd at first, but when you think of words like *wheelbarrow*, it starts to make sense. Remember that this is only common in Old and Middle English and a few Anglicized words from Dutch. \ō\ elsewhere in words can sometimes be *oa* (*loam*, *boast*), but is most commonly *o* (*abode*, *soken*).
» \ü\ tends to be *oo* (*swoon*), *ou* (*foumart*), or *u* (*cruet*).

» \yü\ is usually either *u* or *ew* (*pewter*).
» \ů\ is oftentimes spelled *u* (*butcher*), with a few words using *ou* (*paramour*).

Consonants

» Old and Middle English love using silent *gh*, and words with *ough*, *eigh*, *igh*, and other combinations all tend to derive from these languages.
» If you hear the \k\ sound, use *c* or *ck*. If \k\ is the first sound in the word and you know that the next letter has to be an *e* or *i*, then spell it with just *k*.
» When you hear a "th" sound at the end of a word, be very careful as to note whether it ends in \th\ (as in *think*) or \th\ (as in *this*). The voiceless \th\ will always be spelled with a *-th* (*wreath*, *breath*, *loath*) at the end of words, but the voiced \th\ will be spelled with a *-the* (*wreathe*, *breathe*, *loathe*). This is a very important distinction to make, and it's tripped me up at spelling bee competitions before!
» Z is not that common of a letter in Middle English, so unless it appears at the very start of a word, spell the \z\ sound *s*.
» Some Old and Middle English words have the sound \hw\ in them. If you hear this sound, spell it *wh*.

General

» Old English words tend to be spelled similarly to how most "regular" English words are spelled, so unless it's a rare exception, try to sound the word out and spell it that way.

» Many words from Old and Middle English are also great vocabulary words, so spend some time learning the meanings of these words.

» Some words are considered "pure" Old English, meaning they did not undergo the same Anglicization process that most other words did. Because there are not that many of them, it's worth researching these words and taking the time to learn them individually. Examples include *fyrd*, *gesithcundman*, *hamsocn*, *sceatta*, and *witenagemot*.

» There are a considerable number of Old and Middle English adjectives that spell \-əl\ as *-el*, instead of *-al*. These are exceptions, and they do show up every so often; *charnel* was asked in Round 3 of the 2021 National Spelling Bee. Make a list of these words, because they are some of the weirdest exceptions to standard English.

» \-səl\ at the end of words is *-stle*, which might also feel really odd at first, but you can remember it with words like *bristle*, *nestle*, and *whistle*.

» \-ək\ at the end of words is *-ock*, a Middle English

root that means "small," as in *hillock* and *lassock*.

<u>LATIN</u>

Latin is an ancient Indo-European language that was spoken from the 7th century BC until approximately 700 AD. During this period, it emerged as the official language of the Roman Empire and became the most significant language in Europe. Latin is the mother of all the Romance languages, including Spanish, French, Italian, and Portuguese. Latin was once the primary language of science, law, and religion throughout Europe. This is why the majority of Latin-derived words in English are linked to these subjects. Although Latin is no longer a spoken native language, it continues to be an essential source of vocabulary in English. In fact, about one-third of all the words in the English language are derived from Latin. If you want to master that one-third, there are a few essential rules to familiarize yourself with. Latin usually has quite a few ways of spelling each sound, but you might already be familiar with many of them because of just how many Latin-derived words you have seen in English. Below are some of the key rules to remember, along with some examples and exceptions:

Vowels

» The schwa, \ə\, is by far the most confusing sound to spell in Latin, so let's get that over with first. It can be spelled using every vowel letter, and even combinations of vowels. Here's a few examples: *cardamom, celebratory, falciform, amorous, cumulus, Abyssinia.*

- The best tip for spelling the schwa in Latin is to spell it *i* when you're connecting two roots in the middle of a word. As an example: nearly every Latin word ending in \-əfòrm\ has the ending *-iform*. So, spelling words like *columniform, struthiform,* and *uniform* should be straightforward once you know to use *i* in the middle.

- If you hear the schwa at the end of a word, it is almost always *a* (*antenna, larva,* and *vertebra*). Keep it simple here!

- Additionally, you can try and relate Latin words to other words that you already know of so that you can remember how to spell the schwa. For example, if you were learning the word *caliber*, you could try connecting it with the word *calibrate*, to remember two words at once. Since Latin words are so common in English, you probably already know a lot of them.

SPELLING ANYTHING

» The rest of the vowels in Latin words are very
similar to how you would normally say them in
English: *a* is \a\ (*abacus*) or \ā\ (*abrasive*); *e* is \e\
(*elemental*), \ē\ (*egotistical*), or \i\ at the start of
some words (*emancipation*); *i* is \i\ (*incision*) or \ī\
(*ibex*); *o* is \ō\ (*ovoid*), \ȯ\ (*oral*), or \ä\ (*occidental*);
and *u* is \ü\ (*fluvial*), \yü\ (*usuary*), \u̇\ (*tuberculosis*),
\yu̇\ (*subcutaneous*), or \yə\ (*calculus*). Remember
these pronunciations, because you may come
across a word in which there are two different
pronunciations. As an example, the word *obelisk*
can be pronounced both \ˌä-bə-ˌlisk\ and \ˌō-bə-
ˌlisk\. The first vowel has to be spelled *o* because it
is pronounced both \ä\ and \ō\ in the word.

» Most Latin words in English aren't pronounced
exactly like they were in the original language;
they went through a process called Anglicization,
which means that words became more like
English instead of Latin through centuries of
sound changes. There are a few words where this
process never happened, and so the original vowels
are pronounced differently: *a* is \ä\ (*casus belli*), *e* is
\ā\ (*videlicet*), *i* is \ē\ (*scilicet*), *o* is \ō\ (*a tergo*) and
u is \ü\ (*ius*).

» *Au* is certainly an interesting vowel combination to
learn about. It is usually pronounced \ȯ\, in words

like *au*scultation and *au*tomobile. The best way to remember what words are spelled with *au* and which ones are *o* is to learn the roots that contain those spellings and memorize the ones that don't have roots at all.

» Another important combination to look at is *eu*. *Eu* normally makes the \yü\ sound, as in *feudalism*.

Consonants

» If you ask for the etymology of a word and hear either "Latin from Greek" or "New Latin," then be careful! These words are likely to follow Greek spelling rules instead of Latin ones. We will be learning more about Greek rules later, but this is something you'll need to remember in order to avoid misspelling words that actually follow Greek spelling instead of Latin.

» The \k\ sound is spelled either *c* (*clavicle*) or *cc* (*accusation*) nearly all of the time. If a word has Latin parts that derive from Greek, consider spelling it *ch* (*chiragra*) or *cch* (*saccharine*). Take notes of those words, as well as the very rare occasions where the \k\ sound is followed by \e\ or \i\ and is still spelled with a *c* (*civitas*).

» The \ks\ sound is usually *x* if it's at the end of a word (*multiplex*) and *cc* if it's in the middle and followed by *e* or *i* (*accipiter*).

» The \s\ sound is one of the most confusing consonant sounds to spell in Latin. You can spell it *s* anywhere in the word (*sonic, astringent, cactus*), *ss* in the middle or at the end (*assay, crass*), and you can spell it *c* or *sc* if the following vowel is *e, i,* or *y* (*cenacle, civics, scene, scissile*). Knowing which one it is can often depend on your intuition for spelling, knowledge of roots, and plain memorization of the exceptions.

» There are a few common words that spell the \sh\ sound with an *s*, like *assure,* but \sh\ is most often spelled as *-ti-* (*initial*) or *-ci-* (*beneficiary*), followed by a vowel. We can see this in the endings *-tion* and *-cion*, as in *nation* and *internecion.* The best way to differentiate between which is which is always to ask for alternate pronunciations. *-ti-* is often pronounced \ch\ after consonants (*exponential, quincuncial*) and *-ci-* can sometimes be pronounced \sē\ (*uncial*). Aside from this, learning roots associated with *-ti-* and *-ci-* and connecting related words together are both good ways of dealing with the words you may not get right from the above method alone.

» The \zh\ sound is usually spelled *-si-* (*incision*) and *-su-* (*usual*), followed by a vowel. However, when used after a consonant, *-si-* and *-su-* sound more like \sh\ (*dyspepsia, consensual*).

» The \j\ sound is spelled *g* when followed by the letters *e* or *i*, as in *gesture* or *gingivitis, d* in some cases when followed by *u* and then a consonant, as in *coadunate*, and *j* everywhere else, like in *jactation* or *jurisprudence*.

» The \y\ sound can be spelled *j* in words that have not been Anglicized, such as *jus soli*. In most cases, however, that *j* can be pronounced both \j\ and \y\ (*de jure, juramentum*). In the words that have been Anglicized, you can probably spell \y\ with *y*, as these words don't show up very often.

» Double consonants in Latin do occur quite often, in words like *allative, connotation,* and *error.* A good way of knowing when to use double consonants is getting used to assimilation. Assimilation is when a prefix changes its spelling to match the rest of the word it's attached to. An example is *assimilation* itself; the word used to be *adsimilation*, but the *ds* combo got too hard to say, and so Latin speakers changed it to *assimilation.* The *ad-* prefix became *similar* to the rest of the word. We can see this in words like *attraction* (once *adtraction*), *commemoration* (once *conmemoration*), and *illogical* (once *inlogical*). In the cases where double consonants aren't due to assimilation, you can usually rely on roots and memorization to seal the deal. For example: *millennium* comes from the Latin roots *mille* (thousand) and *annus* (year), which is why it has two double consonants in it.

General

» Whenever you hear the \-əbəl\ sound at the end of a Latin word, you might be very confused on whether to spell it *-able* or *-ible*. The clearest way of figuring out which way to spell it is to relate it to words that are similar, because they will usually end in another suffix that has an *a* or an *i* in it. For example: the word *imitate* ends in *-ate*, which means that *imitable* must end in *-able* to match. The word *credit*, which ends in *-it*, is related to *credible* and *incredible*, so both of those words have the *-ible* ending to match. This works in most cases, but make sure to keep track of words that either don't follow this rule or don't have a related word at all.

» If you hear the \-ər\ sound at the end and the word is a noun, the spelling can either be *-er*, *-or*, or *-ar*. All three of these suffixes mean "a person who does something," so it's important to know the specifics: *-er* is a general ending that derives from Middle English but is used in a lot of Latin words (*calorifier, transducer*); *-or* is a Latin-specific ending used commonly in the ending *-ator* (*elevator*) and the subjects of anatomy (*dorsiflexor*) and law (*testator*); and *-ar* is another Latin-specific ending that is used in a few words you might want to note down (*bursar, commissar*).

» If the \-ər\ sound is used in an adjective, good chances are it's spelled *-ar*, as in *caruncular* and *linear*.

» The \-əs\ sound is another huge trouble spot for spellers! If the word is an adjective, it is almost always *-ous*, but if the word is a noun, there are a few options: *-us* and *-is* are the two key endings. *-us* is the most common ending for nouns derived directly from Latin, like *corpus*, as well as many genus names (the scientific terms for species). *-is* is used with certain words, like *thesis*, as well as other genus names. Additionally, if the word passed through Anglo-French and Middle English before it reached Modern English, then *-ice* is a possibility to consider (*pumice, malice*).

» The \-shən\ ending, which means "action," is usually spelled *-tion*. However, there are many words in which that ending is spelled *-sion* (*ascension*), and even a few with -*cion* (*interne**cion***). I recommend you make lists of those words, since there's not a large number of either.

» Note down what words use -*tious*, -*cious*, and -*ceous* for the \shəs\ sound at the ends of words. -*tious* and -*ceous* relate to characterizations, while -*ceous* is commonly used for plants and animals. If you can identify which one a word comes from, it gives you a huge advantage when you're on stage.

» Nearly every noun in the English language has a plural form: you add -*s* or -*es* to the end of the word. Latin has the same thing, and many of its unique plural forms have made it into the English language.

- When you see a Latin word ending in -*us*, the plural form of that word likely ends in -*i*. As an example: the word *cactus* has the plural *cacti*. Exceptions: *corpus* has the plural *corpora*, and *tempus* has the plural *tempora*.
- When you see a Latin word ending in -*um*, the plural form ends in -*a*. As an example: the word *bacterium* becomes *bacteria* in plural.
- When a Latin singular word ends in -*a*, the plural form is usually -*ae*. Example: the word *antenna* becomes *antennae*.
- Finally, when a Latin word ends in -*is*, the

plural tends to be -*es*. Example: the word *axis* becomes *axes*.

- There are several cases for each of these endings where the word's plural is just the English one (*bonus* → *bonuses*; *coliseum* → *coliseums*; *militia* → *militias*; *brachialis* → *brachialises*).
- This is important to keep track of because these plurals can be pronounced in confusing ways that may trip you up if you're not careful with these endings, so making sure to memorize them is the best way of mastering these words.

» The best part about Latin is that because so many Latin words have entered English, it's very easy to make connections between Latin words and their close English relatives, called cognates. This will help you remember not only the spelling, but in many cases, the meaning too! For example, the Latin word *febrile* is related to the English word *fever*, which is perfect because the word *febrile* means "feverish."

<u>FRENCH</u>

French is a Romance language that evolved from Latin and is primarily spoken in France, Belgium, Switzerland,

and parts of Canada and Africa. Its influence on the English language has been significant, particularly after the Norman Conquest of England in 1066, during which French became the dominant language of the English court, law, and administration. As a result, English absorbed a vast number of French words, especially in areas related to government, law, art, and cuisine. Currently, it's estimated that 30–40% of English vocabulary is derived from French, highlighting its role as one of the most influential languages in the evolution of English.

Out of all the spelling patterns, French is the hardest to learn because of the countless different variations and exceptions to each rule. Below is a summary of French spelling rules:

Vowels

» French is famous for its nasal sounds, which are pronounced with a lowered soft palate to let air pass through your nose—hence *nasal*. If you hear one of these sounds in a word, note that the vowel letter likely has an *m* or *n* after it.

» The \ä\ sound in French is oftentimes just *a*, as in *pâté*, but there are times when it is *o*, such as *solfege*. In these instances, you may have to focus on roots, or connect the word to a related one. Here, *solfege* means the music note system that goes "do-re-mi-fa-sol-la-ti-do," and you can remember this word by connecting with *sol*, one of the notes. Some words spell \ä\ with the letter *e*, especially when followed by *m* or *n* (**empennage, entrepreneur**), and others spell \ä\ with silent letters at the end of words (*alternat, foie gras*), so take note of those.

» French is famous for its nasal sounds, and \äⁿ\ is the first one we will cover. It is usually spelled *en-* and *em-* at and around the start of words, *-ent* and *-ant* at the end, and *an* almost anywhere. *em-* is usually used before the letters *p* and *b* (**empressement, emboîtement**), whereas *en-* is used everywhere else (**en** *carré,* **en***voûtement*). *-ant* is used for adjectives (*beauséant, fainéant*), while *-ent* can be seen primarily in the French noun ending *-ment* (*denoue***ment**, *morcelle***ment**). Words with *an* include **andouille**, **blanquette**, and *Chouan*.

» The \a\ sound is almost certainly *a*. There are a couple words where this sound is spelled *i* because it is followed by the \m\ or \n\ sound (*indienne*).

» The \aⁿ\ sound is usually spelled *in* (*béguin, taste***vin**).

» The \ā\ sound in French is by far the most confusing of any! The most common spelling for this sound is *e* (*éclair*), but there are many times when this is not the case. You will practically always see *e* at the start and middle of words, and you might occasionally see *ai* (*baignoire*) and *ei* (*seigneur*), but it's at the end where things get a bit more confusing. Alongside *e*, you might see *ée* at the end of some nouns and adjectives, such as *pommée*. This happens because *-é* is the masculine past participle ending, whereas *-ée* is the feminine past participle ending. Although to my knowledge, the National Spelling Bee doesn't allow you to ask for these as roots, there is a chance that you can at your local bees, so try asking those roots when you can, because you can use this to your advantage and correctly spell one of the hardest endings in French by just asking for the roots. You can also create mnemonics that reflect whether the word is masculine or feminine in French. Aside from these two, you may also come across the endings *-et*, which is a root that means "small" or "little" as in *beignet*; *-er*, which you can see in words ending in *-ier* (*cahier, semainier*); or *-ez*, which derives from the imperative suffix, showing a command that is given, as in *oyez* and *rendezvous*. Note that *-ez* is not a very common ending, so I'd recommend just learning the words where that ending appears by heart. Finally, you may see *ai* being used as a spelling for \ā\ in words like *aigrette* and *béarnaise*.

» If you hear the \-et\ sound at the end of a French word, there's a high chance to spell it *-ette*. Examples include *baguette, chansonnette,* and *raclette.* This is the feminine ending meaning "small" or "little," and it shouldn't be confused with the masculine form of this ending, *-et*. Luckily, *-et* is usually pronounced \-ā\ (as seen previously), so as long as you note down the instances where it is also pronounced \-et\ (like *clarinet*), you should be good to go.

» The \e\ sound is almost always *e*, such as *echelon*.

» The \ē\ sound is often *i*, as in *critique* and *reprise*, but be careful, and always ask for alternate pronunciations, as they could reveal different spellings. The word *éclair* is an interesting case of this. You may first hear just \ē-'kler\, but ask for the alternate pronunciations, and you will then hear \ā-'kler\ too. The only letter that makes sense in this position is *e*, and so you should spell this word starting with an *e*. The \ē\ sound is usually *ie* at the end of words, as in the ending *-erie* (*coterie, japonaiserie*), but be careful, for there are exceptions such as *coulis* and *gabarit*.

» The \i\ sound is usually just *i*, as in *chiffon* and *fichu*.

Keep it simple and straightforward!

» The \ī\ sound is spelled *aill* in the middle of words (*paillasson*) and *aille* at the end (*mitraille*).

» The \ō\ sound is usually spelled *o*, as in *crochet*, but can occasionally be spelled *au* as in **auteur** and *fabliau*. There are some odd spellings that occur when \ō\ is heard at the end of a word. The most well known of these is *-eau*, as in *border**eau*** and *portmant**eau***. Interestingly, this ending has a special plural form: *-eaux* \-ō(z)\. *-eaux* is sometimes pronounced like \-ō\ (*agn**eaux***), sometimes like \-ōz\ (*chalum**eaux***), and sometimes like both \-ō\ and \-ōz\ (*morc**eaux***). Not to mention, the occasional *-eaus* plural, pronounced just \-ōz\, which is seen in a few Anglicized words such as *gasper**eaus***. This is quite confusing, and although there are times where asking for alternate pronunciations really does help, I recommend you memorize these words, as there are not too many of them and they are easy breeding grounds for misspelling the word when you get it. And *-eau* is not the only example of this; it's the same story for another spelling of \-ō\, *-ot* (seen in *escarg**ot*** and *maill**ot***). This ending has a plural of its own, *-ots* \-ō(z)\, which can be pronounced in up to two separate ways depending on what word you get. There are a few words ending in *-os* \-ō\, such as *apropos* and *malapropos*, but luckily these two words do not have plurals as they are adjectives. When you get a French word ending in \-ō\, be VERY CAREFUL about the pronunciation and ask for the part of speech, because they will tell you if it is a singular noun or a plural noun, and that is the key to deciding whether to add an extra letter at the end or not!

» The \ōⁿ\ sound is almost always *on* (*Bondon*, *garçon*).

» The \ȯ\ sound is most often spelled *o* (*dormeuse*, *estoppel*), and is sometimes spelled *au* (*chauffer*).

» The \œ\ sound, which sounds like a fusion of \ü\ and \e\, is usually spelled with *eu* (*au bleu*, *condrieu*).

» The \ü\ sound is usually spelled *ou* (*mousse*, *choucroute*, *clafouti*), but it can occasionally be spelled *u* (*fondu*) or *ue* (*battue*). \ü\ and \yü\ are pronunciations that generally tend to be spelled *u* as well (as in *voiture* and *cardecu*, respectively), so ask for alternate pronunciations because it may reveal the correct spellings of words like this. At the ends of words, \ü\ can occasionally be *-oux* (*doux*, *roux*) and even *-eux* (*Chartreux*, *tic douloureux*).

SPELLING ANYTHING

» Alongside *u, ou* is also a valid spelling for \ù\, as seen in *tourbillion*, but this spelling does not show up in that many words.

» Some words in French have the \ue\ sound, which sounds like a fusion of \ü\ and \i\, and you can spell this sound with *u* (*muguet*) or *ue* (*bienvenue*).

» An even smaller number of words have the \yü\ sound, which once again can be spelled with *u* (as mentioned above) or *ue*.

» The \ər\ sound at the end of words is oftentimes *-eur* (*connoisseur*). This is a root ending which means "one who does." As an example, the word *connoisseur* roughly translates to "one who knows," which makes sense given the meaning of *connoisseur* is "expert."

» The schwa \ə\ in French can be absolutely anything, so it still relies upon roots and context clues to figure it out. If you can't find a solution to remembering the schwa's spelling, there's a good chance you'll have to memorize it. *C'est la vie.*

» Sometimes, the letter *e* is silent in the middle of a word (*gobemouche, colichemarde, au revoir*). This only happens if there are at least two syllables in the word and the *e* in the middle is not stressed. Don't rely on this for every word though; I recommend you just make a list of these.

Consonants

» The \t\ sound is spelled *t* anywhere in a word (*naïvet*é), *tt* between vowel letters (*coquettish*), and *th* in a couple words you have to memorize (*discotheque*).

» The \k\ sound is spelled *qu* before *e* and *i* (*netiquette*), and *c* everywhere else. If you hear the \k\ sound at the end of words, it's usually spelled *que*, but note the few examples where this doesn't happen, like *caoutchouc*. There are some occasions where French uses *cqu* before *e* or *i* to spell words (*becquerel*).

» The \g\ sound is spelled *gu* before *e* or *i* (**guetapens**, bour**gu**ignonne), *gue* at the end of a word (*ampongue*), and *g* everywhere else (*gaspergou, sagoin*).

» The \s\ sound is *s* at the start of words (*sangfroid*), *ss* in the middle (*paillasson*), and *sse* at the end (*bagasse*). BUT – there are similarities to Latin, in that when followed by *e* or *i*, \s\ can be spelled *c* (*cinquefoil, nacelle, coup de grace*). Some words use *c* to represent \s\ even though it's followed by a letter that isn't *e* or *i* (*facade, limaçon*) – this is because French has a diacritic called the cedilla, which looks like a hook under the *c*. In French, as well as Portuguese, the cedilla makes the letter *c*

SPELLING ANYTHING

sound like \s\ everywhere.

» The \sh\ sound is almost always *ch* at the start and middle of words (***chassis***), and *che* at the end of words (*quiche*).

» The \z\ sound is usually *s*, and appears in the middle of words (*grisaille*), but can sometimes be *z* if it shows up at the start.

» The \zh\ sound is usually *g* when followed by *e* or *i* (***gendarmerie***), *ge* at the ends of words (*camouflage*), and *j* when followed by any other vowel (***jaspé***). *j* can also be pronounced \j\, so if you hear both \ zh\ and \j\ as pronunciations for the same letter, then you should go for *j*. *ge* can also appear in the middle of some words when it is followed by any vowel aside from *e* or *i*, as seen in *bourgeoisie*.

» The letter *w* rarely ever shows up in French. If you hear the \wä\ sound, it's probably spelled *oi* (*boiserie*, *Loire*) If you hear the \w\ sound next to any other vowel, there's a good chance it's spelled *ou*, as in *gouache*.

» The \y\ sound is usually *ill* when preceded by a vowel, as in *paillasson* and *bouillon*.

» The \ny\ sound is oftentimes *gn* in words like *peignoir* and *champignon*.

» French loves its silent consonants! These letters show up primarily at the end of words. Examples include *sangfroid*, *Limoges*, *abat-voix*, *contretemps*, and *chez*. Additionally, the letter *h* is sometimes silent, as in *bonhomie* and *hauteur*.

» Double consonants are also a common sight in French, especially at the ends of words when followed by the letter *e*. Examples include *baguette*, *frappé*, *coiffeuse*.

General

» The most important trick to know about French is that French is a language with gender embedded into its nouns. Every noun is divided into two groups: masculine (male) or feminine (female). The telltale sign of a feminine noun in French is the inclusion of an extra *e* at the end of the word (*mousse, college, promenade, maquette*). Masculine words have no *e* at the end, and if there's a consonant before the *e*, that consonant will usually become completely silent (*chassepot, Cagoulard, gardebras*). This is generally a good way of correctly guessing whether a word has an extra *e* at the end or not (*croquet* \(')krō-¦kā\ versus *croquette* \(') krō-¦ket\). However, it might not help when the word is Anglicized because English doesn't usually silence the last consonant in a word. It also may not help if the word ends in a vowel like \ā\, since it would sound the same with or without the extra *e* (for example, *bouché* and *bouchée* are homonyms). Additionally, as seen above, there are a few cases where even if you don't hear a consonant sound at the end of a word, there is still a consonant letter there—it's just silent. This isn't super common except for cases like *-et*, so don't start spelling French words with random letters at the end; just take notes on the oddballs that spell words this way, and move on with the rest.

» French has an extraordinarily weird plural system. Some words have a SILENT *s* at the end. Every time you see a word that has a silent plural, NOTE IT DOWN and keep practicing that list! These are some of the toughest words in all of the dictionary, and mastering these will save you if you get one at a spelling bee.

<u>GREEK</u>

Before Latin became the dominant language of Europe, that title was held by Greek. An ancient Indo-European language with a rich history, Greek was commonly used as the language of classical philosophy, science, and literature in ancient times. Although it is now only spoken in Greece, the Greek language has had a significant influence on English, particularly in scholastic terminology. Many English words in fields such as biology, medicine, mathematics, and philosophy have Greek roots.

There are several essential rules to keep in mind when it comes to Greek. Similar to Latin, many words have been Anglicized, but there are some distinct differences that you will need to familiarize yourself with. By mastering these key patterns, you'll be well on your way to understanding the language.

Vowels

» Let's start with the schwa \ə\: Again, you can spell the schwa in virtually every possible way in Greek (*desmachyme, genesis, microscopic, sisyrinchium, chamaerrhine*).
  - The connecting schwa between roots in Greek is almost always spelled *o* (*technocratic, zoological*).
  - The schwa at the ends of nearly all Greek words is *a* (*syntagma*).
» The \ə\ sound is spelled with *e, i,* or *y. i* is rather common in words ending in -*sis* (*pneumoconiosis*).
» Many of the vowel sounds are spelled similarly to Latin: \a\ is *a* (*apathy*), \i\ is *i,* and \ō\ is *o.*
» The \a\ sound is *a* almost all of the time (*apathy*). There are a few exceptions where *a* is followed by

a silent *g* (usually in words ending in *-phragm*, like *diaphragm*).

» The \ä\ sound is usually *o* (*collagen, isagogic*), and *a* in the few non-Anglicized words (*moussaka*).

» The \ā\ sound is always *a* in Anglicized words (*abiotic*). There are some cases where \ā\ is *e* in words that have not been Anglicized (*koine*).

» The \ē\ sound is a bit less simple than you might think at first. Yes, in most instances, this sound is just *e* (*edema*), especially at the end of quite a few non-scientific words (*agoge, catastrophe, synecdoche*), but *y* is a common ending for some words too (*monopoly, plutarchy*). Additionally, this sound can be spelled *i* in non-Anglicized Greek words (*pastitsio*), as well as in endings like *-ia* (*ergomania*), *-ian* (*Daedalian*), and *-ion* (*anthemion*). Just like Latin, Greek words ending in *-a* can have the plural *-ae* (*chela* → *chelae; rachilla* → *rachillae*). *Ae* can also show up elsewhere in a few words, like *Achaea* and *aeolian*, and more commonly in the endings to genus names (*-aceae, -aea, -iae, -idae*). *Oe* is also a spelling that exists in the middle of a few words (*Boeotia, polyphloesboean*), and there are a few roots containing it that I encourage you to take note of, like *coel-* (hollow, cavity) and *oen-* (wine).

» The \e\ sound is usually *e* (*metric*), but can sometimes be *ae* (*Aeschylean*), *eg* before *m* (*phlegm*), and *oe* (*oesophagostomiasis*).

» The \ī\ sound is usually *i* (*icosahedron*, *isagoge*), but can also be *y* (*hydrogen*), *ei* (*kaleidoscope*), or *ai* (*daimonion*). *ei* tends to show up in words with the root *eidos* (shape, form), and *y* shows up in roots like *hydro-* (water), *hyper-* (over), *hypo-* (under), *my-* (mouse, muscle), *phyt-* (plant), *psych-* (mind), *pyr-* (fire), and *xyl-* (wood).

» The \ō\ sound is generally *o* in most circumstances (*odylic*).

» The \ü\, \yü\, and \yü\ sounds are oftentimes either *u* or *eu*. Oftentimes, you should pick *eu* because the word has a root containing it: *eu-* (good), *euro-* (Europe), *eury-* (broad), *leuk-* (white), *neur-* (nerve), *pneum-* (air, lung), and *pseud-* (false) are the most common ones. Not every root has *eu* in it: *ur-* (tail) is one example, so pay attention to what roots have *eu* and what roots don't, in addition to words with no important roots that still use *eu* or *u*.

Consonants

» The \k\ sound is most commonly spelled *ch* (*chirality*, *trachea*, *dibrach*). It can also be spelled

SPELLING ANYTHING

c (*carotid, phenocoll*), and in some rare instances, *k* (*katabatic, krasis, moussaka*). Knowledge of roots will save the day when trying to figure out whether to spell a Greek word with *ch*, *c*, or *k*.

» The \f\ sound is spelled *ph* nearly all of the time (*pharmaceutics, chlorophyll, glyph*). Be sure to note down the exceptions to this rule.

» The \t\ sound is usually *t* (*catastrophe*), but can sometimes be *pt* in roots like *pter-* (wing), *ptil-* (feather), *ptyal-* (saliva), and *ptych-* (fold). If *pt* appears in the middle of a word, it might have two pronunciations: one with \t\, the other with \pt\. If this is the case, always spell it *pt* – that alternate pronunciation is a clear indicator of how to spell this sound. There are a small number of words that spell \t\ as *ct* (with a silent *c*). Just make a list of them and keep them in the back of your head.

» The \th\ sound is usually *th* (*apotheosis*), but can be spelled *phth* (*phthiriasis, phthisis*).

» The \n\ sound is usually *n* (*adenoid*) or *nn* (*blennorrhea*), but there are all sorts of options to use at the starts of words. \n\ can be spelled *pn-* in roots like *pneum-* (air); *mn-* in roots like *mnem-* (memory); *gn-* in roots like *gnath-* (jaw) and *gnosis* (knowledge); and *cn-* in roots like *cnem-* (shin) and *cnid-* (nettle). Make lists of the words that start with all of those, because that will come in handy in the chance that spelling bee organizers ask you one of those words.

» The \s\ sound can be spelled *s* (*synchronization*), *ss* (*abyss*), *sc* (*hyoscyamus*), *c* (*cephalgia*), or *ps* (***ps**almodic*). *ps-* in particular can be found in roots like ***ps**almos* (psalm), ***psamm-*** (sand), ***pseud-*** (false), ***psil-*** (mere, bare), ***psor-*** (itch), and ***psych-*** (mind).

» The \r\ sound has three different possibilities: *r* (***r**achis*), *rh* (***rh**odopsin*), and *rrh* (*cata**rrh***). *rh* can be seen in the roots ***rh**abd-* (rod), ***rh**amph-* (beak), ***rh**in-* (nose), ***rh**iz-* (root), ***rh**od-* (red), and ***rh**ynch-* (snout); *rrh* can be seen in the Greek roots *py**rrh**-* (red) and *-**rrh**ea* (flow), as well as variants of the roots for *rh*.

» The \z\ sound is usually either *z* (***z**oology*, ***z**ygote*), *x* (***x**ylophone*, ***x**erostomia*), or *s* (*hypnoti**s**m*).

SPANISH

Spanish is a Romance language that evolved from Latin and is spoken primarily in Spain, Latin America, and parts of the United States. Spanish has significantly impacted English, particularly in areas with a historical Spanish influence, like the American Southwest. Many English words related to food, culture, and daily life have Spanish origins. Because Spanish words originally derive from Latin, many of the spelling rules are quite close to Latin as a result. Spanish is very simple when compared to English, so just learn these rules and you should have no problem breezing through Spanish words in the dictionary!

Vowels

» Spanish vowels are really straightforward. \ä\ is *a*, \ā\ is *e*, \ē\ is *i*, \ō\ is *o*, \ü\ is *u*. These specific sound-spelling correspondences are referred to as the "five-vowel system," and they are mostly standard across many language spelling patterns. Stick to these and you should be good for most Spanish words. Beware of \ä\, however, for it can occasionally be spelled *o*, as in *poncho*, as well as \ē\, which can be spelled *e* especially at the end of words (*coyote, paloverde*).

» The \a\ sound is *a*, the \e\ sound is *e*, the \i\ sound is *i*, the \ȯ\ sound is *o*, and the \u̇\ sound is *u*.

» The \ī\ sound is spelled either *ai* (*copaiba, Taino*) or *ay* (*guayabera, nandubay*).

» Words ending in the schwa, \ə\, are always spelled with *a* (*enchilada*). There are some words with the schwa \ə\ in the middle, but learning Latin roots tends to do the trick for those.

Consonants

» The \ny\ sound is usually just ñ (the n with the tilde), as in *piñata*, but can also be *ni* or *ny* in a few instances.

» The \k\ sound is similar to French – usually *c*, but it is *qu* before *e* and *i*. Examples: *canasta, mescal,* **qu***esadilla,* **qu***inoa.*

» The \g\ sound also bears similarities to French – it's usually *g*, but *gu* before *e* and *i*. Examples: *amigo, gracioso,* **gu***errilla.*

» The \s\ sound is once again a confusing one! It can be *s* anywhere in the word (*sabadilla, ensalada, tapas*), but just like Latin and French, \s\ can be *c* before *e* and *i* (as in *cedilla* and *leoncito*). As of writing this book, there are 25 words that use *ss* and derive from Spanish (like *sassafras*), so make sure to make a list of those. Additionally, there are a few words where \s\ is spelled with the letter *z*, like *azulejo* and *gazpacho*. To deal with this, ask for alternate pronunciations. Most words with *z* pronounced \s\ also have \z\ and sometimes \th\ as options, so whenever you hear that, it's a pretty good sign that it might be spelled with a *z*. For the rest of it, I would once again turn to roots and your knowledge of related words to make the difference here.

SPELLING ANYTHING

» The \ch\ sound is generally *ch*, as in ***chimichanga***.

» The \th\ sound is usually *d*, and only occurs between two vowels (*corri**da***).

» The \h\ and \k\ sounds are almost always *j* (*bru**j**a, e**j**ido*). Only a couple American Spanish words use *h* (***h**icotea*) or *g* (*a**g**itanado*), and even fewer words use *x* (*Oa**x**aca*), so just take notes on what words are the exceptions, and you should be fine.

» The letter *h* itself is usually silent at the start of words, similar to French (***h**abanero,* ***h**ombre*).

» The \w\ sound is an interesting one to spell in Spanish for sure. If \w\ is not preceded by any other consonant, just spell it *hu-* followed by the vowel – ***Hu**elva* and ***hu**isache* are examples. Otherwise, spell it *u*, as in *cuadrilla* and *pueblo*. There is one exception to this rule—the word ***h**oatzin* is pronounced \wä(t)-'sēn\—but just remember that and you should be good.

» The \gw\ sound is usually made with the letters *gu* (***gu**acamole, jag**ü**ey*).

» The *ll* combination in Spanish usually makes the \y\ and \ly\ (*banderi**ll**ero, manzani**ll**o*). Sometimes, the \y\ sound can be spelled *y*, as in ***y**erba maté*, but there are few words with this spelling in place.

» The \r\ sound is always *r* at the start and end of words, but it's in the middle of words where it starts to become an issue. Sometimes the \r\ sound can be *r* in the middle, but it can also be *rr* (*arroz, churro*). Usually, figuring this out comes down to roots and memorization. As an example: the word *tierras* has a double *r* because it derives from the Latin root *terra* (earth), while the word *mirador* has a single *r* because it derives from the Latin word *mirari* (wonder), which is where we get the English word *miracle*.

» Other consonants are generally spelled the same way they would in English, so you shouldn't have too much of an issue dealing with those.

» Double letters are not very common in Spanish, aside from *ll* and *rr*—so make sure to note down any words that use other double consonants.

<u>GERMAN</u>

German is an Indo-European language spoken primarily in Germany, Austria, Switzerland, and parts of Belgium and Liechtenstein. Being a close relative of English, German shares numerous linguistic features and has greatly influenced English vocabulary. German is perhaps most well known for its guttural sounds and its extremely long words, and as a result, its spelling rules might look very confusing and difficult to learn. However, it is actually one of the easiest languages to spell words from once you get used to its rules. German is great at following its rules and staying straightforward, so as long as you learn them, you should be good to go!

Vowels

» \ə\ can be any vowel, but is most often *e* (*abendmusik, scherenschnitte*). However, if the word ends in the \vərst\ sound, spell the ending -*wurst*. There are a couple other German roots that may come in handy when determining how to spell the schwa, but outside of those roots, just spell it *e*.

» \ä\ is either *a* (*backfisch*) or *o* (*oppenheimer*). Occasionally, it is *ah* (*autobahn, Hahnemannism*), but there aren't many of them, so I'd recommend you just learn all of them by heart.

» \ē\ is basically always *ie* (*glockenspiel*) and occasionally *i* (*muesli*).

» \ā\ and \e\ are *e* (*lebensraum, bremsstrahlung*). In the same vein as *ah*, there are a few words where \ā\ is spelled *eh* (*flehmen, Wehrmacht*), and I'd recommend just learning them by heart. Additionally, some words have \e\ spelled as *ä* (*schwarmerei*), but once again, this is not that many.

» \i\ is always *i* (*mittelschmerz*).

» \ī\ is always *ei* (*Weimaraner*).

» \ȯ\ is always *o* (*ostmark*)

» \ō\ is always *o* (***o**berrealschule*), with the exception of a few words that spell it *oh* (*ramdo**h**rite*, *Ro**h**rbordun*).
» \ù\ is always *u* (*ka**p**ut*).
» \ü\ is always *u* (*nachtmusik*), aside from the words where it is spelled *uh* (*schu**h**plattler*, *stromu**h**r*). One exception is *schuetzenfest*, although that has alternate pronunciations \i\ and \ʊe\.
» The \ʊe\ sound is spelled ü or üh in German (*rückumlaut*, *glu**h**wein*).
» \aù\ is always *au* (***au**ftaktigkeit*, *Weltanschau**ung***).
» \ȯi\ is usually *eu* (*schadenfr**eu**de*) and rarely *äu* (*fräulein*).
» Note down every time you see a word with the spellings *oe* or *oeh*. These spellings have many different pronunciations, ranging from \ā\ to \ō\ to \œ\ to even \ə̄\, a lengthened version of the regular schwa. As long as you know what words have these spellings, you should be fine.

Consonants

» \k\ is *k* anywhere in the word (*klaberjass*) and *ck* in the middle and ends (*bockwurst, zwieback*). A few words with *ch* are also pronounced this way (*buchite, dachshund*) The only major exception is *bergschrund*.

» \k̲\ is universally *ch* (*brötchen, sprachgefühl*).

» *qu* can be pronounced all sorts of ways: \kw\, \kv\, and \kf\ are the main ones. Examples include *quellung* \kw\, *quersprung* \kf, kəv\, and *Quincke tube* \kw, kv\.

» \t\ can be *t* anywhere in the word (*knackwurst*) or *tt* in the middle (*mettwurst*), but interestingly, it can also be *d* at the ends of words (*Deutschland, volkslied*).

» \sh\ is essentially always *sch* (*austausch, schläger*), as well as *s* before *p* or *t* (*dehnstufe, strudel*).

» \ch\ is *tsch* (*deutsche mark, zwetschenwasser*)

» \v\ is almost always *w* (*Weissnichtwo, wohlfahrtia*).

» \f\ can be spelled a number of ways. The most common ones are *f* (*Querflöte, flak*) and *v* (*herrenvolk, vorspiel*). *ff* is also used in the middle of words (*dieffenbachia*), and *pf* is used in roots like *kopf* (head) and *pfeffer* (pepper).

» \s\ is usually *s* anywhere in the word (*seligmannite*) or *ss* in the middle (*goldwasser*).

- » \z\ is usually *s* (*desemer, hasenpfeffer*) and sometimes *z* (***z***oisite).
- » \ts\ is most commonly *z* (***z***witterion, fahler***z***), although it can occasionally be *tz* as well (*Carlowi**tz**, gro**tz**en*).
- » \y\ is universally *j*.

ITALIAN

Italian is a language derived from Latin spoken primarily in Italy and parts of Switzerland, with a rich history rooted in the Roman Empire. Although its impact on English is not as pronounced as that of the other languages we've covered, Italian has still contributed significantly, especially in the realms of art, music, and cuisine. Italy's central role in Renaissance culture has had a lasting influence on Western artistic traditions, which is why so many English words relating to the arts come from Italian. Additionally, Italy's focus on cuisine shows through the food words that have made it into English, including plenty of cheeses! Through these influences, Italian continues to enrich English vocabulary, particularly in cultural and culinary spheres. Italian is the closest of the Romance languages to the original Latin language, and so, the rules regarding Italian are rather simple.

Vowels

» The five-vowel system from earlier takes hold for the most part in Italian: \ä\ *a* (*pasta*), \ā\ *e* (*piacevole*), \ē\ *i* (*broccoli*), \ō\ *o* (*solenne*), and \ü\ *u* (*gruppetto*).

» \ä\ doesn't have to be *a* in all circumstances; *o* is also a common spelling (*coppa*). Figuring out which is which is dependent on your intuition and root knowledge.

» *i* isn't the only spelling for \ē\. *e* is also a regular occurrence, especially at the ends of words (*fettuccine*).

» Many other rules from the other Romance languages in particular also apply here: \a\ is *a* (*polacca*), \e\ is *e* (*secco*), \i\ is *i* (*diminuendo*), \ȯ\ is *o* (*oratorio*), and \u̇\ is *u* (*villeggiatura*).

» When a word has \yü\, it's spelled *u* (*fumarole*). The only exceptions are words containing the Italian root *più* (more), which derives from Latin *plus*.

» The schwa \ə\ is usually *a* at the end of words (*pancetta*), but it can be any letter anywhere else in the word (*contrapunto, mountebank, movimento, amoroso*). Again, rely on roots and related words to figure this out, because there are no hard rules on how to spell the schwa at the start or in the middle of an Italian word.

» The dotted schwa \ə̇\ is usually spelled *i* (*pimento*), with occasional *e* (*regatta*).

Consonants

» The \k\ sound is usually *c* (**cappelletti**, *pococurante*), however there are plenty of words where this is not the case. \k\ can sometimes be spelled *ch* in the middle of a word, usually when followed by *e* or *i* (*marchesa*, **chiaroscuro**). In the middle of words, \k\ can be *cc* (*acciaccatura*, *bocca*) or *cch* when followed by *e* or *i* (*gnocchi*, *orecchiette*). Whether to spell with one *c* or two, is again up to roots and context, but I recommend taking notes of words that spell \k\ with *cc* and *cch*, as they are assuredly fewer in number than *c* and *ch*.

» The \g\ sound is somewhat similar – it's usually *g* (*fata morgana*, **garibaldi**), but *gh* before *e* or *i* (*fughetta*, *larghissimo*).

» The \ts\ sound is usually *zz* (*pizza*, *tazza*).

» The \sh\ sound faces a similar predicament – it's normally spelled *sc* before *e* or *i*, but must be spelled *sci* before any other vowel (*a rovescio*).

» The \ch\ sound is also quite confusing too. It's spelled *c* when followed by *e* or *i* (*cellist*, *seicento*), but is spelled *ci* before any other vowel (**ciabatta**).

In the middle of words, it can be spelled *cc* before *e* or *i*, and *cci* before other vowels (**acci**accatura) – figuring this out relies on memorizing words with *cc* and *cci*.

» The \j\ sound is very similar to the \ch\ sound in spelling. It can be spelled *g* and *gg* before *e* or *i* (**G**enovese, arpe**gg**iated), but has to be spelled *gi* or *ggi* before other vowels (**gi**allolino, appo**gg**iatura). It's just as confusing as the \ch\ sound, and the solution is the same—memorizing what words have *gg* and *ggi*.

» The \z\ sound is spelled *s* (Parmesan, sgabello).

» The \s\ sound can be spelled either *s* (virtuoso) or *ss* (meno mosso).

» The \ny\ sound is *gn* (lasagna), and likewise the \ly\ sound is *gli* (imbroglio). Be wary, for there are a couple times where \ny\ is spelled *ni* (carabiniere) and where \ly\ is spelled *li* (alto-rilievo).

» The \y\ sound is generally *i* when it follows a consonant and precedes a vowel; **chi**avetta is one example.

» The \w\ sound is generally *u* when it follows a consonant and precedes a vowel, as in egualmente.

» The rest of the consonants are very similar to Spanish, so as long as you remember which ones are different in Italian, you are good to go.

» Italian loves its double consonants. This is due in part to assimilation and the original Latin roots, leading to words like *affrettando*, *appassionato*, *mantelletta*, and *trattoria*.

General

» Because it is a Romance language, Italian shares the majority of its roots with Latin, so knowing what Latin roots appear in Italian words is crucial. You can see this with the Italian suffix *-abile* \\-äbəlā\\, which comes from the Latin ending *-able*, as in *ballabile* and *lamentabile*.
» The plural forms of nouns in Italian are also different, just like in Latin and French. This time, they are a lot simpler:
  - Words ending in *-o* and *-e* have their plurals end in *-i* (*concerto* → *concerti*; *campanile* → *campanili*).
  - Words ending in *-a* have their plurals end in *-e* (*chiavetta* → *chiavette*).
  - Note that the last consonant will change spelling to match the following vowel (*bottega* → *botteghe*; *baiocco* → *baiocchi*).
  - Some words in Italian don't have these plurals, but spelling bee organizers like asking words that are out of the ordinary, so make sure to keep these forms in your head.

DUTCH and AFRIKAANS

Dutch, a language spoken primarily in the Netherlands and Belgium, has had a noticeable impact on English, especially in areas related to trade, navigation, and technology. As another sister language to English, Dutch is the source for many English words that we use every day, including terms related to trade and commerce. Afrikaans is a language evolved from Dutch, spoken primarily in the former Dutch colony of South Africa, and its history in the Southern Hemisphere has led to slight spelling changes that are worthy to note. Here are the rules for spelling words from Dutch and Afrikaans:

Vowels

» The schwa \ə\ can be spelled with nearly any letter (*calamander, Barnevelder, dominie, avondbloem, kurvey*).

» Like Italian loves double consonants, Dutch and Afrikaans love double vowels! Double vowels in these languages include *aa* for \ä\ (*raadzaal, Afrikaans*), *ee* for \ā\ and \ē\ (*Keeshond, geeldikkop*), and *oo* for \ō\ and \ü\ (*boomslang, voortrekker*).

» The \ä\ sound can be spelled *a* (*platteland*), *o* (*bontebok*), or the aforementioned *aa*.

» The \a\ sound is always *a* (*boomdassie*).

» The \ā\ sound is *e* (*Nederlands*) or *ee* (*kaneelhart*).

One major exception you may want to note is *drostdy*.

» The \ē\ sound is either *i* (*waterzooi*), *ie* (*galsiekte*), or *ee* (*keest*).

» The \i\ sound is essentially always *i* (*gifblaar*, *wildebeest*).

» \ī\ can be spelled *ij* (*Wijs method*), *i* (*isinglass*), and occasionally *y* (*mynheer*). *ij* is by far the most common, but *i* appears in words that have been significantly Anglicized.

» \ō\ can be spelled *o* (*kokerboom*), *oo* (*hoogaars*), and *ou* (*vetkousie*).

» \ȯ\ is consistently spelled *o* as in *landdrost*.

» \ü\ is spelled *oe* (*pampelmoes*) and *oo* (*rooibok*).

» \au̇\ is *ou* (*kabeljou*) or *ouw* at the end of words (*vrouw*).

» The letter combination *ui* can be pronounced a number of ways: \ü\ (*spruit*), \ī\ (*muishond*), \ȯi\ (*sandkruiper*), \ā\ (*uitlander*), and \ə\ (*muid*) are all possible. The best way of dealing with all of these is just memorizing the words that have *ui* in them, since there aren't that many.

Consonants

» \k\ is almost always *k* (**kingklip**). Take careful notes when you see words where \k\ is spelled *c* (**caam**).

» \k̲\ is usually *g* (**berghaan**). This is because in Dutch and Afrikaans, the letter *g* makes a similar guttural sound.

» \t\ can be *d* at the ends of roots and words (**veldschoen**), but is most commonly *t* (**Amsterdammer**) or *tt* (**witteboom**).

» \sk\ can be spelled *sk* (**skaamoog**) or *sch* (**schooner**).

» \ch\ is spelled *tj* (**kommetje, uintjie**), especially in the *-tjie*/*-tje* suffix, which means "small."

» The \f\ sound is usually either *f* (**konfyt**) or *v* (**drilvis**).

» \y\ is *j*, as seen in *jacopever*.

» Double consonants in Dutch and Afrikaans are a regular sight, and you can usually tell when to use double consonants through the same intuition you would use for English words. The word *dubbeltje* would be pronounced differently if it had only one *b* instead of two. Use this principle to help you decide.

General

» When Dutch words look more English, they tend to be more common: *school, stripe, staple*, and *floss* are all Dutch words. So the tendency for words like these is to spell them like regular normal English words. Your best bet to tell Anglicized words apart from native Dutch ones is either to watch out for either Middle English, Old English, or Anglo-French in the etymology, or to learn which words are which beforehand.

» A lot of Dutch and Afrikaans words have English relatives, and this can help you remember the spellings and the meanings of certain words. For example, the word *platteland* is related to the English word *flatland*, and that's very similar to the meaning of *platteland*. The word *rijsttafel*, a rice meal, derives from the Dutch words *rijst* and *tafel*, which are related to the English words *rice* and *table*.

» Many Dutch roots show up multiple times throughout the dictionary, so here are a couple of the most important ones: *bok* (deer), *boom* (tree), *hout* (wood), *klip* (cliff), *kop* (head), *siekte* (disease), *uit* (out), *veld* (field), *volk* (people, folk).

<u>PORTUGUESE</u>

Portuguese, a Latin-derived language spoken primarily in Portugal and Brazil, has had a moderate influence on English vocabulary, especially during the Age of Exploration in the 16th and 17th centuries. As Portuguese sailors and explorers established trade routes and colonies around the world, they introduced new terms into English, especially related to navigation, geography, and food. Because Portugal and Spain are located next to each other on the map, their two languages are closely interlinked and they share many spelling patterns. However, Portuguese also has a few unique rules that are crucial to know in the chance you get a Portuguese word at your bee. Let's take a look at some of them:

Vowels

» The schwa can once again be spelled in every way possible (*Fernambuco, ouricury, arrojadite*).
  • *a* is a common ending, like Spanish.
» Four of the five vowels in the five-vowel system have returned: \ä\ *a* (*sargasso*), \ā\ *e* (*auto-da-fé*), \ē\ *i* (*vinhatico*), and \ō\ *o* (*toston*). See below for more details on \ü\, because *u* is *not* the most common spelling for that sound in Portuguese.
» \ā\ can be *e* as mentioned above, or *ei* (*freijo*). *ei* is most commonly seen in the *-eiro/-eira* endings, which are related to English *-er* and mean the same thing: "one who does."
» \e\ is always *e* (*centavo*).
» \ē\ is *i* as stated above, although *e* is a possibility (*cabreuva*).
» \i\ is almost always *i* (*nicuri*).

- » \ī\ is either *ai* (*copaiba*) or *ay* (*tayra*).
- » \ȯ\ is usually *o* (*mordisheen*).
- » \ü\ is spelled either *o* (*louro*), *ou* (*acajou*), or *u* (*babassu*). If you hear an alternate pronunciation \ō\, chances are it's likely *o* or *ou*, but otherwise, all three are possible. The most common one is *o*, so I'd urge you to learn the ones that are not spelled that way.
- » \au̇\ can be spelled either *au* (*berimbau*) or *ao* (*pardão*). I recommend you to learn the spellings of the -*ao* words, as there are fewer of them.
- » Nasalization can happen in Portuguese, as seen in words like *vintem*. When that happens, spell the next letter with an *m* if the vowel is the last sound in the word or if the following sound is \p\ or \b\, and spell it with an *n* in every other case. The exception to this general rule are words like *tostão*, *João Pessoa*, and words starting with *São*.

Consonants

- » The \k\ sound is similar to Spanish in that it is *c* in most instances (*caixinha*), but *qu* before *e* and *i* (*alcornoque*, *jequitiba*).
- » The \g\ sound is once again similar: *g* in most cases (*burgao*), but *gu* before *e* and *i* (*seringueiro*).
- » The \gw\ sound is formed with the letters *gu*

(**gu**axima, jara**gu**a).

» The \s\ sound can be spelled *s* (*escudo*), *ss* (*imbiru**ss**ú*), or *c* (*icica*). *c* can be used before all vowels, not just *e* and *i* (*cachaça*). This is because Portuguese has the same cedilla that French does.

» The \z\ sound is spelled with a *z* (*fazendeiro*).

» Whenever you hear the \th\ sound in Portuguese, it is spelled *d* (*fa**d**o, feijoa**d**a*). This is one of the key similarities that Portuguese has with Spanish.

» The \j\ sound is *j* (*jambolan, jupati*), with the exception of *genipap, gentoo, giboia,* and *Magellan*.

» The \sh\ sound can be spelled *ch* (*chibigouazou, lorcha*) or *x* (*abacaxi, maxixe*).

» The \zh\ sound is spelled *j* (*jaboticaba*).

» In Portuguese, the \ny\ sound is spelled *nh* (*piranha, marinheiro*). This can be seen in the ending *-inho/-inha*, which means little.

» The \ly\ sound is spelled *lh* (*chocalho*).

» Just like Spanish, Portuguese does not have many double letters. The ones that occur the most often are *rr* and *ss*.

General

» Making connections between Portuguese words and their English, Latin, or Spanish counterparts is a great way of knocking out multiple words at once! As an example: The Portuguese-derived word *senhor* is related to the Spanish-derived word *señor* and the Latin-derived word *senior*.

INDO-IRANIAN LANGUAGES (Sanskrit, Hindi, Persian)

Indian languages, including Sanskrit and Hindi, alongside Iranian languages like Persian, have significantly enriched the English language with a diverse collection of words, reflecting the region's extensive history of cultural, trade, and colonial connections with the English-speaking world. Words from Hindi, often related to everyday life, food, and cultural practices, entered English during the British colonial period in India. Sanskrit, like Latin, is the mother of numerous South Asian languages, and its deep influence on religion, philosophy and literature is reflected in its contributions to the English language. Persian, which is spoken in Iran, has had a significant influence on English as well, thanks to the former heavy British trade association with Iran. Heavy Anglicization from when these words were brought into English has resulted in similar language patterns for all three of these languages, so let's take a look at the rules associated with them:

Vowels

» The schwa \ə\ is usually *a* (*bharata natya, paratha, daftardar*), with occasional appearances of *u* in Anglicized words (*cummerbund*) and *ah* at the ends of words (*ayatollah*). *ah* and *u* primarily appear in Hindi and Persian words, with *a* being almost ubiquitous in Sanskrit.

» The dotted schwa is usually *i* (*malikana*).

» The same five-vowel system from above applies to many words from these languages: \ä\ is *a* (*acharya*), \ā\ is *e* (*chela*), \ē\ is *i* (*Parsi*), \ō\ is *o* (*mofussil*), and \ü\ is *u* (*Hindustani*). However, there has been a significant amount of Anglicization in words from Hindi and Persian, and so this system does not apply to every word.

» \ä\ can be spelled *a*, as mentioned above, *o* (*pottah*), and *ah* (*Brahman*). *a* is by far the most common, as well as the standard in words directly from Sanskrit, so go with *a* if you're feeling unsure.

» \e\ is always *e* (*ekka*).

» \ē\ is either *i*, as mentioned above, *ee* (*purree, sittringee*), or *y* (*dacoity, sepoy*).

» \i\ is simply *i* (*chillumchee*).

» \ī\ is *ai* in most cases (*chaitya*). Exceptions include *ryot* and *ryotwar*.

» \ȯ\ is *o* (*halalcor, koftgari*).

- » \ü\ is either *u* or *oo* (*langooty*). Which one it is depends on how much the word has been influenced by English, which you usually have to memorize.
- » \u̇\ has the same spelling patterns as \ü\: either *u* (*dasturi*, *gulmohar*) or *oo* (*hookum*).

Consonants

- » Many consonant sounds in these languages are generally spelled as they sound, but there are often variations with an extra *h* after them. For example: \p\ can be both *p* (*pachisi*) and *ph* (*phansigar*); \b\ can be both *b* (*bahuvrihi*) and *bh* (*bhalu*); \t\ can be both *t* (*tatpurusha*) and *th* (*thanadar*); \d\ can be both *d* (*dasturi*) and *dh* (*dharma*); \k\ can be both *k* (*kuttar*) and *kh* (*akhundzada*); and \g\ can be both *g* (*nargileh*) and *gh* (*gharial*).
- » Aside from *k* and *kh*, a small fraction of words from these languages spells \k\ with *c* (*cuttanee*). *kh* is more common in Persian than in Sanskrit or Hindi, although *k* is the most common in all three languages.
- » In addition to *d* and *dh*, the \d\ sound can be spelled with *ddh* (*Buddhist*). Nearly all of these words start with *buddh-* and have to do with Buddhism, so as long as you know that and the

words *siddha* and *sraddha*, you'll be good to go.

» \sh\ is spelled *sh* (*dharmshala*).

General

» Because of how much words from these languages have been Anglicized, some words are spelled just like regular English. Case in point: *budgerow*, *cutcherry*, and *tilyer*.

» One root you might want to know is *-dar*, which means "holder." This can be seen in words like *bhumidar*, which means "landholder," and *thanadar*, which translates to "military post holder" or "head of a military post."

<u>RUSSIAN</u>

The Russian language's impact on English can be seen through the lens of the Cold War, in which words relating to government, agriculture, space, and literature became commonplace in English. The following are the spelling rules regarding this language.

Vowels

» \ə\ at the end of words tends to be *a* (*babushka*, *taiga*). Aside from that, the schwa can be spelled nearly every possible way, as usual (*fersmanite*, *slivovitz*).

- » \ä\ can be spelled *a* (*apparatchik*) or *o* (*oprichnik*). Think about whether the word makes sense if spelled with an *a* or an *o*, and if you aren't sure, *a* is more common.
- » \e\ is *e* (*feldsher*).
- » \ē\ can be spelled *y* at the ends of words (*kolinsky*, *perwitsky*) as well as the usual spelling of *i*.
- » \i\ is *i* (*holluschick*).
- » \ō\ is *o* (*lovozerite*).
- » \ü\ is *u* (*sevruga*).

Consonants

- » Most of the consonants are spelled as they sound, but there are a few exceptions. \k\ is usually spelled *k*, but in rare circumstances can be spelled *kh* (*kolkhoznik*, *Stakhanovite*). There isn't really a specified technique for knowing which ones these are, so I'd recommend just memorizing the ones that are spelled *kh*.
- » \sh\ is *sh* (*Bolshevik*), \ch\ is *ch* (*chetvert*), and \zh\ is *zh* (*muzhik*).
- » \y\ is *j* (*jeremejevite*).

General

- » A common root found in Russian is *-nik*, which derives from Yiddish and means "one associated with."

ARABIC

Many goods and ideas traded with the Western world have appeared as Arabic words borrowed into English. Below are some of the rules for spelling words from Arabic.

Vowels

» \ə\ is usually *a* in Arabic words. However, there are plenty of words where \ə\ is spelled with the *-ah* ending (*ayatollah, dahabeah*), so make sure to take note of those words.

» \ə̇\ is spelled *e* (*rebab*).

» \ä\ is spelled *a* (*imam*) and can occasionally be *o* in some Anglicized words (*albatross, tarragon*).

» \a\ is always *a* (*azoth*).

» \ē\ is primarily spelled *i* (*khamsin*).

» \i\ is spelled *i* (*majlis*).

» \ō\ is written *o* (*Sokotri*).

» \ü\ can be spelled *u* (*sambuk*) and *ou* (*ouguiya*). *ou* is especially common when the word in question relates to North Africa or a part of the world formerly colonized by France; as an example, *ouguiya* is the currency of Mauritania.

» A few words have a silent *h* after a vowel, like *bahr, ihram,* and *mihrab*. Make a list of these words, as they are exceptions to the general rule regarding vowels.

Consonants

» The \k\ sound is usually *k* (*kaffiyeh*), but can be *kh* in a few words (*mukhtar*). The \k\ sound can also be *q* in a few instances (*qiyas, Qutb*), and is occasionally spelled c in Anglicized words (*carmine*).

» Although \f\ is almost always *f*, there are a few occasions in which it is spelled *ph* (*nenuphar*), and this is because of Anglicization. There are very few times when this happens, so make sure to make a list of those words.

» Arabic tends to have double consonants in words that have been Anglicized. Some examples include *foggara, kissar,* and *diffa*.

» The other consonants are spelled how they sound, so words from Arabic should not be a huge problem consonants-wise.

General

» A lot of Arabic words have exactly three consonants in them, because almost all native Arabic roots are three consonants long; for example, *ihram, sayyid, sharif,* and so on.

» Many Arabic words have been modified heavily, going through multiple different languages before reaching English, and so they have slightly different spelling rules compared to more recent words that still carry the original Arabic romanization. Whenever you come across an Arabic word, make sure you note down which type the word is.

» Many Arabic words start with *al-*, because it means "the" in Arabic. As an example: ***al**batross*, ***al**cohol*, ***al**gebra*, and even ***ad**miral* all come from this origin. Note that some words do come from this Arabic root, but do not start with *al-*; see *elixir* as an example.

SCANDINAVIAN LANGUAGES (Norwegian, Swedish, Danish, Icelandic)

Scandinavian languages like Norwegian, Swedish, Danish, and Icelandic are part of the Germanic language branch, and therefore a close relative to English. They're spoken in northern Europe, and all of them originate from Old Norse, an ancient language which has given English plenty of base vocabulary. Additionally, Scandinavian languages have provided words relating to maritime activities, reflecting the long Nordic presence in the fishing world. The following are the spelling rules for these languages.

Vowels

» The schwa \ə\ is usually spelled either *a* or *e* (*smorgasbord, aebleskive*).

» \ä\ and \a\ are both spelled *a* (*bankskuta, Dannebrog*).

» The \ā\ sound is *ey* in Icelandic (*eyrir*).

» \e\ can be spelled either *e* (*marmennill*) or ä (*hälleflinta*).

» \ē\ is spelled *i* (*appetitost*).

» \i\ can either be spelled *i* (*rosemaling*) or *y* (*syssel*). *i* is vastly more common, so just memorize the ones with a *y*.

» \ī\ can also be spelled with an *i* (*iberite, struvite*) or *y* (*mysost, rype*).

» \ō\ is spelled *o*, as expected (*finnesko*).

» \ü\ can either be spelled *u* (*lutefisk*) or *o* (*hambo*). *o* is a Swedish-specific spelling of this sound, while *u* is a more general Scandinavian spelling.

» \œ̄\ is a lengthened version of \œ\, and it is spelled *o* in Scandinavian languages (*smørrebrød, stød*).

Consonants

» \k\ is spelled *k* (*kornerupine*), with the sole exception of words with the name *Kjeldahl*.

» \ch\ is usually *ch*; *gyttja* and *tjaele* are the only two Scandinavian *tj* words.

» \z\ is spelled *s* (*berserker*), in much the same way as English.
» \y\ is spelled *j* (*fjord, ijolite*); ***gyttja*** and ***gjetost*** are two exceptions.
» The remaining consonants are pronounced the way you would expect, which makes sense because these languages are some of English's closest relatives.

HEBREW and YIDDISH

Hebrew and Yiddish, both languages with deep roots in Jewish history and culture, have made notable contributions to English vocabulary. Hebrew is the official language of Israel and the only language in history to experience a successful large-scale revival, and it has introduced several words, primarily related to religion, into English. Yiddish, a Germanic language spoken primarily by Ashkenazi Jews worldwide, has contributed a variety of expressions to the English language. These languages are very similar in their spelling rules, so let's review them both.

Vowels

» The \ə\ sound can be spelled with most of the vowels (*yeshiva, menorah, tefillin, Beelzebub*). *ah, a* and *e* are the most common spellings at the ends of words, and *e* and *u* are usually considered middle-word schwas. Your intuition will once again come into play here!

- Many words from these languages end with the spelling -*ah* (*megillah*), but some of them end in just -*a* (*yenta*). It is CRUCIAL to remember the list of Hebrew and Yiddish words ending in just -*a*, since they are the minority of words and can easily trip you up if you're not careful. These words don't have many clues to suggest whether it's spelled -*a* or -*ah* from the pronunciation alone, so learning the words will take care of that.

» \ä\ can be spelled *a* (*landsmanshaft*), *o* (*nimrod*), and *ah* (*havlagah*) in Hebrew and Yiddish. *o* is very common in words of Biblical origin, while *a* is common in non-Biblical terminology. See above for information about -*ah* and -*a*.

» \a\ is spelled *a* (*Lazarus*) essentially all the time.

» \ā\ is spelled *e* in non-Biblical terms (*ashre*) and *a* in Biblical words (*David*).

» \e\ is spelled *e* as usual (*luftmensch*).

» \ē\ can be spelled *i* (*bedikah*) or *e* (*Nehemiah*) in non-Biblical and Biblical words, respectively.

» \i\ is spelled *i* (*bar mitzvah*).

» \ī\ tends to be spelled *i* (*Goliath*) in Biblical terms, and *ai* and *ei* elsewhere (*Adonai*, *fleishig*).

» \ō\ is spelled *o* everywhere (*Cohen*).

» The spelling of \ȯ\ is usually *o* in Hebrew and Yiddish (*lokshen*, *piroshki*).

» \ü\ is spelled *u* (*hallelujah*, *rugelach*) in both Hebrew and Yiddish.

Consonants

» \k\ can be spelled *k* (*apikores*) or *g* (*milchig*). *k* is never silent like it is in English's *kn*. The 2013 National Spelling Bee winning word was *knaidel* \ kə'nādəl\.

» \ḵ\ is spelled *ch* (*hechsher*) or *h* (*holishkes*). The most common spelling is *ch*, so go with that if you're not feeling sure.

» \t\ is almost always spelled with *t* (*teruah*, *yahrzeit*); however, some Hebrew words also end in *-th/-t* (*berith/berit*, *tehinnoth/tehinnot*). This *-th/-t* can be pronounced \t\, \th\, and/or \s\ depending on the word, which may sound confusing at first. However, these extra pronunciations may actually clear up the spelling of the last sound as *-th/-t*. The best way to avoid potential confusion, however, is just to memorize the words where this happens.

» \ts\ is spelled *tz* in Hebrew and Yiddish (*hamotzi*, *blintze*).

» \sh\ can be spelled *sh* in both languages. *sch* is an extra spelling found primarily in Yiddish words (***sch***lockmeister*).

General

» Words in Hebrew have specific plurals that might be worth noting.
- The most common plural form is general, in which words have *-im* \-im, -əm\ added to them (*cherub* → *cherub**im***; *maskil* → *maskil**im***). Some words have irregular changes before adding *-im* at the end (*seder* → *sed**arim***; *shegetz* → *shk**otzim***), and you will just have to memorize these in case one of them gets asked.
- The second most common one is for words ending in *-ah* \-ä, -ə\, whose endings become *-oth*/*-ot* \-ōth, -ōt, -ōs\ in the plural form (*kapparah* → *kappar**oth***/*kappar**ot***; *prutah* → *prut**oth***/*prut**ot***).
- The last plural we'll cover is a primarily Yiddish plural form for words ending in *-el* or *-l* \-əl, -l\. These words become pluralized by changing their endings to *-lach* \-lək\ (*chremsel* → *chrems**lach***; *kichel* → *kich**lach***).
- Many words just use the regular English

plural endings of *-s* and *-es*, while some words instead have no difference between the singular and plural forms.

JAPANESE

Japanese is spoken in Japan, perhaps the furthest possible part of the world from England! Even still, Japanese has made notable contributions to English vocabulary, especially in technology, cuisine, and culture. Luckily, Japanese spelling rules are pretty straightforward, so let's take a look:

Vowels

» The schwa \ə\ is most often *a* (*hiragana*), but it can also be *e* (*akebi*), *i* (*norimon*), or *o* (*kimono*).

» \ä\ is spelled *a* in nearly all cases (*kanji, katakana*), with the exception of words like *honcho*, which have an *o* in its place.

» \ā\ is mostly spelled *e* (*bon-seki, matsutake*), but can also be spelled *ei* (*keiretsu, nisei*). One important exception you might be asked is *bokeh*.

» \e\ is spelled *e* (*Nichiren*) virtually all the time.

» \ē\ is spelled *i* in most cases (*shiatsu, Meiji*), but sometimes, the letter *e* can represent \ē\ at the ends of words (*karaoke, netsuke*). There are only two words where \ē\ is spelled *ii*: *shiitake* and *shikii*.

- » \i\ is almost always *i* (*kikumon*, *pachinko*).
- » \ī\ is spelled *ai* (*bonsai*, *zaibatsu*).
- » \ō\ is *o* (*aikidoi*, *gyokuro*).
- » \ü\ is spelled *u* (*ponzu*, *shubunkin*). \ü\ is also spelled *u* (*butsudan*, **urushiol**).
- » Some words have silent vowels in them (*nunchaku*, *netsuke*). These two examples have alternate pronunciations that make it obvious, but it's important to not get confused by these silent pronunciations.

Consonants

- » In Japanese, nearly every sound has only one spelling. Don't go overboard with it unless you are 100 percent confident it's an exception. \k\ is *k* (*koan*), \g\ is *g* (*geisha*), \j\ is *j* (*judo*), \sh\ is *sh* (*shakuhachi*), \ch\ is *ch* (*nunchaku*), and so on. Keep it simple!
- » That said, one sound that might not be as simple as you think is the \s\ sound. In most cases, it's spelled *s* (*sashimi*), but in some words, it is spelled *ts* (**tsunami**). Luckily, nearly every word with this spelling also has an alternate pronunciation of \ts\, so you should be fine when spelling words with the \s\ sound.
- » Double consonants are not that common in Japanese, so make sure to take notes every time you see one. Examples include *tenno, issei, hokku.*

CHINESE

Chinese has contributed several words to the English language, particularly related to food and philosophy. Centuries of contact with Western powers has led to English having a sizable chunk of Chinese vocabulary, so let's review the spelling patterns that define it:

Vowels

» The schwa \ə\ is spelled *u* in the middle of words like *subgum* and *a* at the end of words like *pela*. Aside from that, the schwa does not make many appearances in Chinese, and the few that remain can usually be told apart from each other through context and intuition.

» \ä\ is spelled *a* (*ahung, chanoyu*), except for a few spelled *o* (*pongee, bonze*).

» \a\ is always *a* (*tangram*).

» \e\ is virtually always *e* (*renminbi*).

» \ē\ can be spelled *i* (*pidan*) or *ee* (*urheen*).

» \i\ is usually spelled *i* (*dim sum*).

» \ī\ is *ai* (*saimin*) or *y* (*sycee*). Note down the words that spell it *y*, since those are exceptions.

» \ō\ is *o* (*boba, senso*).

» \ü\ in particular can sometimes be *oo* (*oolong*), as well as *ou* (*souchong*), aside from the more common *u* (*kung fu*).

Consonants

» One odd feature of the Chinese language is that because it is not natively written in a Latin script, it has to be Romanized, and as a result, there are two Romanizations for the Chinese language. One of them is the more commonly used system called Pinyin, which is used for most geographical names, alongside other more recently borrowed words. The other is an older, lesser-used system called Wade-Giles, which is much more confusing and is still used in many words. This discrepancy means that some sounds are spelled in very odd ways depending on the word: \b\ can be *p* (*pai-hua*); \d\ can be *t* (*tuchun*); \g\ can be *k* (*Kwangtung*); \j\ can be *ch* (*Choukoutien*); and \sh\ can be *hs* (*hsin*). I encourage you to make a list of words with these differences because they are very confusing when you get to spelling them.

» The \ch\ sound is very often *ch* (*bok choy*), but can occasionally be *q* (*qigong*), alongside other words. Similar case with the \sh\ sound, which is very often *sh* (*shar-pei*), but can occasionally be *x* in geographical terms (*Xiamen*), as well as *hs* at the start of a few words (*Hsia*).

NATIVE AMERICAN LANGUAGES

Native Americans are the original inhabitants of North America, whose terminology has been brought into English to describe the nature and geography of the continent, alongside their culture. There are many different indigenous languages with different names, but they all follow the same basic concept: The words have been heavily changed to match the spelling rules of English, Spanish, or French.

This happens because when colonizers came from Europe to the New World, they only understood very little of what Native Americans were speaking. As a result, indigenous words were mispronounced by colonists and altered over time to match the spelling patterns of the language the colonists spoke—either English, Spanish, or French. This is why a Native American word like *bayou* ends in the letters *ou*—because that's how you'd spell the \ü\ sound in French, which is where this word passed through before reaching English. The word *coyote* ends in the letter *e* because that's how you'd spell the \ē\ sound in Spanish. And it's why words like *allocochick*, *sasquatch*, *wampum*, and *werowance* are all spelled with such English-like spelling rules. These words were all picked up by English colonists and written with Anglicized spelling. English is the most common of the languages for which this happens, but if you happen to come across words from indigenous languages, try to pinpoint what language the word might have gone through before it reached English, if at all, and remember to keep it simple throughout; that is your best bet at spelling Native American words correctly.

GAELIC
(Irish and Scottish)

Irish and Scottish are the two main Gaelic languages, spoken in Ireland and Scotland. As the closest languages to English geographically, their contributions to English were established in the 12th and 16th centuries respectively. Because of the prominence of English within the United Kingdom, Gaelic words in English have gone through plenty of Anglicization in their spelling. These languages have a very interesting set of rules to learn, so let's go over them.

Vowels

» Many of the vowel patterns will resemble the patterns of Old and Middle English, due to those languages' heavy influence on the words English borrowed from Irish and Scottish.
» The schwa \ə\ can once again be spelled in any way possible (*coronach, esker, usquebaugh, fili*).
» \ä\ can be spelled *a* (*ballogan*) or *o*. It all relies on

context and your understanding of regular English spelling rules.

» \a\ is *a* as usual (*clarsach*)
» \e\ is spelled *e* (*fillebeg*).
» \ē\ can be spelled in several different ways: *ie* (*collieshangie*), *ee* (*gombeen*) and *y* (*bonnyclabber*) are three of the most common. Using your intuition is key to spelling this sound right.
» \i\ is *i* (*Firbolg*).
» \ō\ is *o* (*camog, ullagone*).
» \ȯ\ is also *o* (*jorram, ogham*).
» \ü\ is usually *oo* (*bosthoon, gillaroo*). It can also be spelled *eu* (*cranreuch*), *u* (*duniewassal*) or *ui* (*cruiskeen*).

Consonants
» \k\ is spelled *c* (*cashel*) or *ck* (*shamrock*). *ck* usually only exists in the context of words ending in *-ock*.
» \k\ is always spelled *ch* (*beallach*).
» \g\ is simply *g* (*Gaeltacht*).
» \sh\ is spelled *sh* (*shanachie, drisheen*) or *s* (*aisling, feis*). Far more words have *sh* than *s*, so note down every time you see a word where \sh\ is spelled *s*.
» \th\ is spelled either *dh* or *dd* (*fuidhir, skean dhu, rinkafadda*).

General

» One common ending for Irish and Scottish words is *-een*, which means "little," as in *avourneen*.

» Some un-Anglicized words have significantly different spelling patterns than the rest of Irish and Scottish. Unless it is easier for you to learn the rules for these on a different basis, I recommend just learning those words by heart. Examples include *bodhran, caoine, ceilidh, flaith, taoiseach*, and *uilleann pipe*.

WELSH

Welsh is the other major language spoken in the UK, besides English, Irish and Scottish. Most Welsh speakers live in Wales, and their language has not gone through as much Anglicization as the Gaelic languages. As a result, Welsh is very unique in the rules it has, so let's take a look.

Vowels

» \ə\ can be anything (*galanas, pendragon, Cymry*).

» \ä\ is generally spelled *a* (*cynghanedd*). \a\ is also spelled *a* (*amgarn*).

» \e\ is always *e* (*cromlech*).

» \ē\ is spelled *i* (*corgi*) and *y* (*clogwyn*).

» \i\, like \ē\, is also spelled *i* (*kistvaen*) and *y* (*gwyniad*).

» \ī\ is spelled *ai* (*plygain*).
» \ü\ might seem simple, but oddly enough, it's actually spelled *w* (*cwm*). One word even has *wy* as a combination to spell \ü\ (*tyl**wy**th teg*).

Consonants
» \k\ takes on the spellings *c* (*coracle*) and *ch* (*lech*). The aforementioned *kistvaen* is an exception to this rule.
» Like Irish and Scottish, \k\ is spelled *ch* (*cromlech*).
» The \th\ sound is spelled *dd*, just like the Gaelic languages (*eiste**dd**fod*, *cywy**dd***).
» \v\ is spelled *f* (*tref*) in addition to *v* (*kistvaen*).

General
» Welsh has some interesting plurals to review:
  • *cynghanedd* → *cynganedd**ion***
  • *englyn* → *englyn**ion***
  • *cywydd* → *cywydd**au***

POLYNESIAN LANGUAGES
(Hawaiian, Maori, etc.)
Polynesian languages are spoken in some of the islands in the Pacific Ocean, most prominently in Hawaii and New Zealand. These languages have contributed several words to English vocabulary, particularly in relation to

the Pacific Islands, their culture, and natural environments. These rules are fairly simple, so let's go through them:

Vowels

» The schwa \ə\ can be spelled in several different ways, but the most common is by far *a* (*aholehole*, *kakapo*). Some other \ə\ spellings include *e* (*toheroa*) and *u* (*whapuku*).

» The vowels are incredibly straightforward in Polynesian. With almost zero exceptions, the five-vowel system takes hold. \ä\ is *a* (*amakihi*), \ā\ is *e* (*faipule*), \ē\ is *i* (*kia ora*), \ō\ is *o* (*koromiko*), and \ü\ is *u* (*motu*).

» The \e\ sound is spelled *e* (*elepaio*).

» The \ē\ sound is either *i*, as listed above, or *e* (*pahoehoe*).

» The \i\ sound is *i* (*piripiri*).

» The \ī\ sound is spelled *ai* (*haeremai*).

» The \aü\ sound is spelled either *au* (*maunaloa*) or *ao* (*omao*). *au* is consistently more common than *ao* across all Polynesian languages, so if you're unsure of which to use, go with *au*.

Consonants

» There are far fewer consonants in these languages than there are in English, and they're all spelled completely regularly, with a few exceptions. \k\ is *k*, \t\ is *t*, \s\ is *s*, and so on.

» The \w\ sound is usually *w* (***wahine***). In some Maori words, it can be spelled *wh*, but usually, these words will have an alternate pronunciation of \hw\, which makes it clear that it's *wh* (as in *porokai**wh**iria*). Make a list of words where *wh* is only pronounced \w\, since it's one of the most confusing parts of the otherwise-simple Polynesian languages.

» In Maori, the \f\ sound spells *wh* (***wh**akapapa*) in addition to \(h)w\. In other Polynesian languages, the \f\ sound is simply spelled *f*.

» The letter *h* is silent when it is in the middle of many Maori words, like *kohekohe*. At the start of words, it is pronounced \h\ (***h**ei-tiki*), as it is in every other Polynesian language (***h**imene*, *kono**h**iki*).

<u>EPONYMS</u>

Eponyms are words that are derived from people's names. For example: *sandwich, diesel, boycott,* and *nicotine* are all eponyms because they were all derived from the name of a person. Whenever you hear an eponym at the spelling bee, pay very close attention to the language of origin. The pronouncer might tell you that the word originates from a specific part of the world, and this can help you because the names from those regions are spelled according to the language patterns. For example, an eponym from France, like *Foucauldian*, is more likely to follow French spelling rules, whereas an eponym from Germany, like *Nietzschean*, is more likely to follow German spelling rules. Be wary because this isn't always the case, and there are many situations in which names, especially older ones, have been Latinized (became more like Latin) before entering English. As an example, the word *Linnaean* derives from Swedish taxonomist Carl von Linné, whose name was Latinized to Carolus Linnaeus, which is why *Linnaean* has the letters *ae* in it.

GEOGRAPHICAL

Geographical terms are essentially place names, like cities, towns, states, regions, and countries. There are plenty of these types of words, and at first, they might seem confusing to wrap your head around! My best tip for these is to pay attention to the definition and/or language of origin. At least one of these will contain the country or general location of the place name, and from there, you can deduce what the language of origin is most likely going to be. For example, places like *Querétaro* and *Hermosillo* come from Mexico, so you should spell them using Spanish spelling patterns. Also, remember to use the pure, non-Anglicized spelling rules for these languages, because most place names have been borrowed into English directly; for example, Dutch place names like *Haarlem* and *Rijswijk* follow non-Anglicized, pure Dutch rules.

<u>UNKNOWN</u>

Words of unknown origin are perhaps the most confusing ones to learn, since there's no one set of rules that fits the majority of them. There are about 2,000 words of unknown origin in the English language, and I highly urge you to memorize as many of them as you can! However, if you get a word of unknown origin and have no clue how to spell it, I have three steps to follow: 1) see if there's other languages listed in the origin; 2) listen to the definition for any country or part of the world from which you can deduce the language; and finally, 3) if all else fails, go for normal English spelling rules. Words like *alveloz* have "unknown origin" at the end, but Brazilian Portuguese is listed before that, which is an indication to spell it like it's Portuguese. Words like *ajowan* and *mayeng* have definitions relating to India, which implies that you should spell it similarly to words from Hindi or Persian. Finally, words like *hootenanny* don't have either of those indications, and so you should be more inclined to spell these kinds of words like normal English. Even following these steps, there will still be plenty of exceptions that do not make any sense (*cailcedra*, *chappaul*, *hooley-ann*, *sieva bean*), and there is no choice but to memorize these. So, take notes every time you see one of these—it can come in very handy if you get one at your bee.

IRREGULAR

Words that are listed as "irregular" are perhaps some of the weirdest words in the dictionary – I bowed out at the 2022 National Spelling Bee to the word *samlet*, which comes from the word *salmon* (note the silent L in the middle) BUT is listed as "irregular from *salmon* + *-let*" in the language of origin. The only true way to know these words is to memorize them, and if you type "irregular" into the Etymology field in *Merriam-Webster Unabridged's* Advanced Search, you will get a complete list of over 1100 words that are listed as "irregular." Be careful with these, because you never know when you will come across one of these words at your bee.

ONOMATOPOEIA/IMITATIVE

Onomatopoeia is when words are named for the sounds that are associated with their meaning. Examples include *meow*, *bowwow*, and *swoosh*. These words almost always follow English spelling rules, with the exception of imitative words that went through other languages before entering English. For those words, just spell it using those languages' spelling rules. Two examples are *bokmakierie* (which is Afrikaans, from imitative) and *quiaquia* (which is American Spanish, from imitative). The easiest way to search these words up is by typing "imitative" into the Etymology field in Advanced Search. This gives you a list of nearly 800 onomatopoeic words as of the time of writing this book.

CHAPTER 6

Root Directory

PNEUMONOULTRAMICROSCOPICSILICOVOL-
CANOCONIOSIS. IT'S ONE OF THE longest words
in the dictionary, referring to a lung disease caused by
inhaling very fine silica dust, and I've spelled this word
on national TV with the legendary comedian Mr. Steve
Harvey! You've probably seen a clip of a six-year-old
me spelling this word on a stage next to Mr. Harvey, on
YouTube or TikTok, and now I want to share with you
the SECRET to how I spelled it.

The secret is… I broke the word into parts. This
long word, *pneumonoultramicroscopicsilicovolcanoconiosis*,
is made up of several smaller portions, called ROOTS,
that we can learn individually in order to master the
full word. We can divide it into *pneumono-ultra-
micro-scopic-silico-volcano-coni-osis. pneumono-* is a Greek
root meaning "lung," *ultra-* is a Latin root meaning

"beyond," *micro-* is a Greek root meaning "small," *-scopic* is a Greek root meaning "seeing," *silico-* derives from the word "silica," *volcano* is just the English word for "volcano," *coni-* is an obscure Greek root meaning "dust," and *-osis* is a Greek root meaning "condition" or "disease." So, all in all, *pneumonoultramicroscopicsilicovolcanoconiosis* is a "lung-related beyond-microscopic silica volcanic dust disease," a lung disease caused by inhaling very fine silica dust particles. What we just did here is break a word down into ROOTS – small parts from different languages that make it easy to remember the full word, and its meaning.

If you memorize roots and their corresponding information, you will be able to spot them in plenty of different words, especially when the word has to do with the meaning of the root. You can confirm this in a real spelling bee by asking for these roots during your turn. If you think some part of the word you've been given comes from a root, then provide the root, its language of origin, and its meaning, and ask the judges if the word comes from that root. As an example, for the word *pneumonia*, you could ask: "Does this word come from the Greek root *pneumo-* meaning 'lung'?" The judges would then respond with "Yes" or "You're on the right track," indicating that the root I referenced can be found in the word's etymology. The root, language, and meaning all have to be correct for the judges to tell you yes, which is why it is so important to learn that information for each root. Luckily, these roots are in so many words that you can easily associate many roots with at least one of their corresponding examples.

Below, I've compiled over 200 of the most important roots you need to learn, along with some examples so you can see how these roots appear in context. Many of these roots have evolved into different languages from the original source (Latin roots are written differently in French, Spanish, Italian, etc.), and examples are provided so that you can recognize these situations. I urge you to memorize the following roots because they will be a key asset in your journey to the National Spelling Bee!

Akash's Word List

1. **a-/an** L. & Gk. not – **a**biotic, **a**historical, **a**specific
2. **ab-** L. from, away – **ab**normal, **ab**rogate, **ab**solve
3. **-able** L. capable of – account**able**, desir**able**, trust**able**
4. **acanth-** Gk. spine – **acanth**ocyte, **acanth**opterygian, **acanth**osis
5. **acar-** Gk. mite – **acar**iasis, **acar**ology, **acar**ophobia

6. **-aceous/-acean** L. relating to - crust**acean**, aren**aceous**
7. **acet-** L. vinegar
8. **acou-** Gk. hearing – **acou**stic
9. **acr-** Gk. top, height
10. **acu-** L. needle
11. **ad-** L. toward
12. **adelph-** Gk. brother
13. **aden-** Gk. gland – **aden**ocarcinoma
14. **adip-** Gk. fat
15. **aer-** Gk. air
16. **afr-** L. African
17. **agath-** Gk. good
18. **-age** Fr. process
19. **-agog-** Gk. leading – dem**agogue**, is**agoge**, ped**agogy**
20. **agro-** Gk. agriculture
21. **-al** L. relating to
22. **alb-** L. white
23. **alg-/-algia/-algy** Gk. pain – neur**algia**, nost**algia**
24. **ali-** L. wing
25. **all-** Gk. other
26. **allel-** Gk. each other
27. **alt-** L. high
28. **ambi-** L. both

SPELLING ANYTHING

29. **ambly-** Gk. blunt – **ambly**opia
30. **amm-** Gk. sand
31. **amph-** Gk. both
32. **-an** L. relating to
33. **ana-** L. up, back, again – **an**ode
34. **andr-** L. man
35. **anem-** Gk. wind
36. **angio-** Gk. blood vessel
37. **anglo-** L. English
38. **anis-** Gk. unequal
39. **ancyl-/ankyl-** Gk. curved – **ancyl**ostomiasis
40. **annu-** L. year – **annu**ity, **annus** horribilis
41. **ano-** Gk. upward
42. **-ant** ME. one who does
43. **ante-** L. before – **ante**penultimate
44. **anth-** Gk. flower – chrys**anth**emum
45. **anthrop-** Gk. human
46. **anti-** L. against
47. **apo-** L. away
48. **aqui-/aqua-** L. water
49. **-ar** ME. relating to
50. **arachn-** Gk. spider – **arachn**ophobia
51. **arch-/archae-/arche-/archi-** Gk. principal, original
52. **arct-** Gk. north
53. **arthr-** L. joint

54. **astr-** Gk. star
55. **atm-** Gk. vapor – **atm**osphere
56. **aud-** L. sound – **aud**ible
57. **aur-** L. ear
58. **aur-** L. gold
59. **aut-** Gk. self – **aut**omatic, **aut**omobile
60. **bar-** Gk. heavy – **bar**ometer
61. **bath-** Gk. deep
62. **ben-** L. good – **ben**efactor
63. **bi-** L. two
64. **biblio-** Gk. book – **biblio**kleptomania
65. **bio-** Gk. life
66. **blast-** Gk. bud – myo**blast**
67. **bov-** L. cow – **bov**ine
68. **brachi-** L. arm
69. **brady-** Gk. slow – **brady**cardia
70. **brevi-** L. short – **brevi**ty
71. **bronch-** Gk. throat
72. **bront-** Gk. thunder – **bront**ophobia
73. **bry-** Gk. moss – **bry**ology
74. **bucc-** L. cheek – **bucc**al
75. **cac-/kak-** Gk. bad – agatho**kak**ological, **cac**ophony
76. **call-** Gk. beautiful
77. **calor-** L. hot – **calor**, oxy**calor**imeter
78. **carcin-** Gk. crab, cancer – **carcin**ogenic

SPELLING ANYTHING

79. **cardi-** Gk. heart – **cardi**ac
80. **carp-** Gk. fruit – **carp**ophagous
81. **cata-/kata-** Gk. down – **cata**strophe, **kata**batic
82. **caud-** L. tail – bi**caud**al
83. **caul-** L. stem – **caul**iflower
84. **cent-** L. hundred – **cent**ipede
85. **chron-** Gk. time – ana**chron**ism, **chron**ic
86. **circum-** L. around – **circum**vent
87. **contra-/counter-** L. against – **contra**band
88. **coel-/cel-** Gk. hollow – **coel**om
89. **demi-** ME. half – **demi**-glace, **demi**god
90. **dia-** Gk. through – **dia**meter, **dia**pason
91. **dict-** L. say – **dict**ionary
92. **dis-** L. bad – **dis**aster
93. **duc-/duct-** L. lead – aque**duct, duct**ile
94. **dyn-** Gk. power – **dyn**amic
95. **dys-** Gk. bad – **dys**functional
96. **eco-** Gk. habitat – **eco**logy, **ek**istics
97. **epi-** Gk. upon – **epi**center
98. **eu-** Gk. good
99. **eury-** Gk. broad – **eury**thermal
100. **fac-** L. do – **fac**ile
101. **fore-** ME. in front of – **fore**warn
102. **form-/-iform** L. shape – **nuci**form
103. **fort-** L. strong – **fort**itude
104. **fract-** L. break – **fract**ure

105. **gam-** Gk. marriage – mono**gamous**
106. **-gon** Gk. angle – hexa**gon**
107. **graph-/-gram** Gk. write – phono**graph**
108. **hemi-** Gk. half – **hemi**sphere
109. **hetero-** Gk. different
110. **homo-** Gk. same
111. **hydr-** Gk. water – an**hydr**ide, cleps**ydra**
112. **hyp-** Gk. below – **hypo**crisy
113. **hyper-** Gk. above – **hyper**active
114. **iatr-** Gk. physician – **iatr**ogenic
115. **in-** L. not – **il**logical, **ir**responsible
116. **in-** L. in, into – **in**flammable
117. **inter-** L. between – **inter**national
118. **intra-** L. within – **intra**mural
119. **intro-** L. inside – **intro**spective
120. **-ject** L. throw – ob**ject**
121. **jud-/jus-** L. judge – **jud**icial, **jus** soli
122. **kilo-** Gk. thousand
123. **leuk-/leuc-** Gk. white – **leuk**emia
124. **log-** Gk. word – **logo**rrhea
125. **-logy** Gk. study
126. **lum-/lumin-** L. light – **lumin**ance
127. **lyt-/lys-/-lyze** Gk. kill – cryptana**lysis**, para**lyze**
128. **mach-** Gk. war – logo**machy**
129. **macr-** Gk. large – **macr**oeconomics
130. **mal-** L. bad – **mal**evolent

131. **-mania** Gk. obsession
132. **matr-** L. mother – **mater**nity
133. **-meter** Gk. measure – **kilo**meter
134. **micr-** Gk. small – **micr**oscope
135. **mis-** ME. bad – **mis**spell
136. **miso-** Gk. hate – **mis**anthrope, **miso**gyny, **miso**neism
137. **mit-/miss-** L. send – ad**mit**, sub**miss**ive
138. **mnem-** Gk. memory – **mnem**onic
139. **mono-** Gk. one – **mono**mer
140. **morph-** Gk. shape – **morph**ology
141. **mort-** L. death – memento **mori, mort**uary
142. **multi-** L. many – **multi**plex
143. **neur-** Gk. nerve – **neuro**n
144. **-nomy** Gk. law – eco**nomy**
145. **non-** L. not – **non**chalant
146. **-nym** Gk. name – syno**nym**
147. **oen-** Gk. wine – **oen**omel
148. **ortho-** Gk. straight – **ortho**dontist
149. **-osis** Gk. condition, disease – hypn**osis**
150. **over-** ME. over – **over**whelm
151. **pan-** Gk. all – **pan**oply
152. **para-** Gk. beside – **para**gon
153. **patr-** L. father – **patr**iarchal
154. **peri-** L. around – **peri**meter
155. **-phile** Gk. love – logo**phile**, oeno**phile**,

philately, **phill**umenist

156. **-phobia** Gk. fear – agora**phobia**
157. **phon-** Gk. sound – tele**phone**
158. **phot-** Gk. light – **phot**osynthesis
159. **phyl-** Gk. tribe – **phyl**ogeny
160. **phyt-** Gk. plant – hydro**phyte**
161. **pneum-** Gk. air – **pneum**oconiosis
162. **poly-** Gk. many – **poly**saccharide
163. **port-** L. carry – tele**port**ation
164. **pre-** L. before – **pre**game
165. **pro-** L. earlier – **pro**active
166. **psamm-** Gk. sand – **psamm**ophile
167. **pseud-** Gk. false – **pseud**onym
168. **psych-** Gk. spirit – **psych**iatric, **psych**ology, **psych**e
169. **pter-** Gk. wing – **pter**odactyl
170. **ptil-** Gk. feather – **ptil**osis
171. **ptyal-** Gk. saliva – **ptyal**in
172. **quadr-** L. four – **quadr**iplegic
173. **re-** L. again – **re**write
174. **rhod-** Gk. red – **rhod**odendron, **rhod**opsin
175. **-rrhea/-rrhoea** Gk. flow – dia**rrhea**, logo**rrhea**
176. **rog-** L. to ask – ar**rog**ant, inter**rog**ation, pre**rog**ative
177. **-scope** Gk. see – micro**scope**
178. **semi-** L. half – hemidemi**semi**quaver, **semi**colon

SPELLING ANYTHING

179. **sen-** L. old – **sen**ile
180. **soph-** Gk. wise – **soph**omore
181. **stat-/-static** Gk. stand – bacterio**static,** lova**stat**in
182. **stroph-** Gk. turn – **stroph**e
183. **sub-** L. under – **sub**space
184. **super-** L. over – **super**annuation
185. **syn-** Gk. together – **syn**chronization, **syn**cope, **syn**ergy
186. **tachy-** Gk. fast – **tachy**cardia
187. **techn-** Gk. technological – **techn**ocratic
188. **tele-** Gk. far – **tele**gram
189. **tetr-** Gk. four – **tetr**agrammaton
190. **the-** Gk. God – **the**omachy, **the**osophy
191. **therm-** Gk. temperature – **therm**ostat
192. **trans-** L. across – **trans**ition
193. **ultra-** L. beyond – **ultra**sonic, **ultra**violet
194. **un-** L. not – **un**-American
195. **under-** ME. under – **under**estimate
196. **uni-** L. one – **uni**fication
197. **ven-** L. come – **ven**ire
198. **vert-/vers-** L. turn – a**vers**e, in**vert**ebrate, **vers**us
199. **vet-** L. old – inve**vet**erate, **vet**eran
200. **vid-/vis-** L. see – ad**vis**e
201. **vol-** L. wish – **vol**ition
202. **vol-** L. fly – **vol**itation

203. **vor-** L. devour – carni**vor**ous, loca**vore**
204. **xen-** Gk. foreign – **xen**ophobia
205. **xiph-** Gk. sword – **xiph**oid
206. **xyl-** Gk. wood – **xyl**em, **xyl**ophone

*Abbreviations:
L. - Latin | Gk. - Greek | Fr. - French
ME - Middle English

CHAPTER 7

Vocabulary Tips

VOCABULARY ROUNDS PLAY A CRUCIAL role at the National Spelling Bee, and depending on your area, you may be asked vocabulary questions at the regional level too. This is why it's important to study vocabulary in addition to spelling. Below, I've laid out some information about how vocabulary questions work and how you can prepare for them.

Why Is Vocab Useful?

Spelling bees include vocabulary (word meaning) questions because they test your comprehensive understanding of language, not just your ability to spell. In doing so, the spelling bee goes beyond simply memorizing words to understanding their meanings, origins, and usage. Knowing the meaning of a word is often directly tied to its correct spelling, as understanding roots, prefixes, and suffixes helps decipher the word's structure. Vocabulary questions also assess your grasp of word usage and context, which are essential language skills. Additionally, vocabulary rounds make the competition more well-rounded by evaluating both spelling accuracy and language comprehension. This ensures that you are not just memorizing words but also engaging deeply with their meanings and origins, fostering a richer appreciation for language. Preparing for vocabulary questions not only expands your word base but also equips you to use these words effectively in daily life.

How Vocabulary Rounds Work

At the National Spelling Bee, the second round of every phase of competition (Preliminaries, Quarterfinals, Semifinals, Finals) is an oral vocabulary round. When it's your turn, you are given your word and asked to select the correct meaning of that word from 3 choices. The time limit for these questions is 30 seconds, which may not seem like much; however, the word and the answer choices are the only information you get, which means that you have most of the time to think through the answer. You have to recall the chosen answer in full. If the answer for the word *clover* is "A: a plant with three-sided leaves," you would be required to say that in full instead of just "A."

At your regional bee, it may differ depending on the rules. Some bees have a preliminary test with multiple-choice vocabulary questions, while others have oral rounds like the National Spelling Bee. The format of questions may also be different. The National Spelling Bee directly asks for the meaning of the given word (like "A *chauffeur* is..."), but other bees may ask questions pertaining to other aspects of the word's meaning (like "A *chauffeur* most likely uses which of the following?", "If someone is a *chauffeur*, they..." or "Which of the following would best be described as a *chauffeur*?"). Many bees, like my regional bee, do not ask vocab questions at all, so make sure to look up more details about your bee or contact your regional bee organizers so that you know exactly how vocab questions will be conducted, if at all.

What Words Are Good Vocab Words?

Of course, not *every* word you come across is a good vocabulary word, just like not every word is a good spelling one. That said, there are specific categories of words that are much better for vocabulary than others, and I have listed some important ones for you to review in the following sections.

Common Terminology

Whenever you hear someone use a word you are unfamiliar with, make sure to note it down, because it could be a good vocab word. Spelling bee organizers are looking for vocabulary words that you would reasonably expect to see in the real world, so if you can gather these types of words, you will have a great foundation.

Onomatopoeia

Onomatopoeia is common not just in spelling rounds, but in vocabulary rounds, too. Spelling bee organizers like asking these kinds of words because it challenges spellers to think about the association between the word and the object—for example, the onomatopoeic words *clunker* (an old piece of machinery; an unsuccessful thing) and *yawp* (to bawl; to complain) were asked in vocabulary rounds at the 2024 National Spelling Bee. Again, searching "imitative" in the Etymology field in *Merriam-Webster Unabridged's* Advanced Search is the best way of finding these words, so take full advantage of it and learn the meanings of these words, too!

Compound Words

Compound words consist of two or more words that, together, have a unique meaning. Examples include *blueberry*, *runway*, and *website*. In some cases, these compound words have meanings completely different from their component parts, and these are the ones you want to focus on the most. One example is *backwater*, which has very little to do with *back* or *water*, and actually means "an isolated place." Words like these are not obvious at all, which makes them appealing to organizers who want difficult or confusing vocab words to ask.

Eponyms

Eponyms, which I described at the end of Chapter 5, can also be good vocab words. Take, for example, *Machiavellian*, which means "characterized by political cunning, duplicity, or bad faith." This word is named after Niccolò Machiavelli, an Italian philosopher during the Renaissance who is famous today for his belief that it was worth it to be cunning and deceiving if the end result was good. These words are commonly used because their meanings are not very obvious—in other words, you have to memorize the connection between them.

Vocab Preparation Tips

Learning vocab is much more reliant on memorization than spelling, but there are still a few tips and tricks that I'd like to share with you in case there are vocab questions or rounds at your local bees.

Understand the Word's Origin

Understanding why the word you're studying has its meaning is probably the easiest way of learning the meaning. Take the example of *blackball*—it means "to veto or vote against something," and that's because the word is named after an old system of voting in which you would vote against something by casting a *black ball* into the ballot box. If you can learn more about the origins of the word you're studying, it provides great context and can prevent you from plainly attempting to memorize every vocab word in the dictionary.

Think about Roots

The roots in a word are another straightforward way of correctly answering vocab questions. The word *acrophobia* may seem confusing to learn at first, but you can break it down into its parts: Greek *acro-* (height) and Greek *-phobia* (fear). Thus, *acrophobia* is the fear of heights. It's combining simple roots like these that will give you a massive edge in vocab rounds.

Relate to Similar Words

If you can associate the word you've been asked with a similar word, it provides another path to getting the meaning correct. By etymology, something that is *irredeemable* cannot be redeemed; it can be as simple as that. In a similar vein, the word *nonpartisan* comes from the word *party*, which is why it means "not affiliated with a political party; neutral." In contrast to the previous examples, some words may seem like opposites but are actually synonyms. Take note of words like *inflammable* and *invaluable*, which are synonyms for *flammable* and *valuable*, respectively.

Additionally, if you can recall similarities between words of different languages, it can also greatly help you in vocab rounds. For example, the Spanish-derived word *frigorifico* means "slaughterhouse for frozen meat," which makes sense because its direct Latin counterpart, *frigorific*, means "cooling or freezing." These direct comparisons make it easy to associate words that you know well with words that you don't.

Eliminate Incorrect Answer Choices

Spelling bee organizers often include incorrect answer choices that closely resemble the correct word in spelling. As an example, the word *treatise* may have wrong answer choices that actually mean *treaty* or *treats*, and many spellers trip up because they confuse the meanings of those words with the correct answer. If you can recognize and eliminate these wrong answer choices, it can narrow down the possible answers to two or even just one! This kind of word association is yet another massive tool you can use to select the right answer.

Infer the Meaning through Etymology

Language of origin is not information you can ask for during vocab rounds, but you may still be able to infer some common themes by guessing the word's language of origin through spelling patterns. Words like *fettuccine* or *parmigiano*, which are Italian and follow Italian spelling rules, relate to pasta and cheese because those are classic parts of Italian cuisine. In the same way, French words like *chardonnay* and *sauvignon blanc* are about wine because those wines are from France. If you can guess the etymology by using the spelling patterns, it can help you eliminate some obviously wrong choices; as an example, a word like *rejoneador*, which is Spanish, clearly does not have anything to do with customs practiced in Asia. (In fact, *rejoneador* is the term for a type of bullfighter. Bullfighting is a common theme among Spanish words, so keep track of those!)

I want to emphasize the importance of Chapter 5 because it contains details about the types of words you can expect for each language, and this is valuable information that can come in handy for vocabulary questions.

CHAPTER 8

Strategies for Spelling Words Onstage

STEPPING ONTO THE SPELLING BEE stage is a moment filled with anticipation, excitement, and nerves. With the spotlight shining and the audience watching, every word presents both a challenge and an opportunity. Success in this high-pressure environment depends not only on knowing how to spell but also on having the right strategies to approach each word with confidence and precision.

This chapter explores the essential tools and techniques to navigate the unique demands of spelling onstage. From managing the mental pressure to effectively using your resources—like asking for the word's origin, definition, or part of speech—we'll cover the strategies that top spellers use to turn uncertainty into clarity. You'll learn how to analyze tricky pronunciations, recognize patterns and roots, and maintain focus under the intense glare of competition.

Whether you're a seasoned competitor or stepping into the spotlight for the first time, mastering these strategies will help you approach each word with poise and determination, giving you the edge needed to succeed on the Bee's biggest stage. Let's dive into the methods that will transform your preparation into performance-ready confidence.

Dealing with Nervousness

Let's address the elephant in the room: nervousness! When you're on stage, it's completely normal to feel those butterflies in your stomach—it's a sign that you care about doing well. The key to handling those nerves is learning how to channel them into focus rather than letting them take control. Start by taking slow, deliberate breaths before and during your turn to calm your heart rate and bring clarity to your thoughts. Visualize yourself succeeding onstage and remind yourself of the hard work you've put into preparing. Positive affirmations like, "I'm ready for this" or "I can handle this word" can help keep your mindset upbeat and confident. Most importantly, center your attention entirely on the task at hand: the word you've been presented with. Block out the audience, your competitors, and everything else in the room, and focus on the pronouncer and the word itself. This moment is about you and your ability to tackle that one word, so let it take center stage in your mind.

Equally important is learning to enjoy the moment. The Spelling Bee is not just a test of your skills but also a celebration of language and learning. Allow yourself to appreciate the experience—the excitement, the camaraderie with other spellers, and the thrill of being onstage. If you feel stressed, think of it as a chance to show how much you've learned rather than a make-or-break situation. Smiling, even slightly, can help release tension and remind you to have fun. Finally, keep things in perspective: One word doesn't define you. Treat every word as an opportunity, stay present in the moment, and trust in your preparation. With a relaxed approach, you'll perform at your best and create memories to treasure long after the competition ends.

Handling the Word

After all your preparation, it's finally time to step up to the microphone and spell your word. In that moment, everything narrows to a single focus: the word. How you approach and manage your time onstage can make all the difference in your performance.

Handling your word onstage is more than just spelling—it's about strategy, focus, and composure. From asking questions to breaking the word into manageable parts, the way you approach your word can improve your chances of spelling it correctly. In this section, you will learn about the strategies I used to analyze and spell words under pressure.

Perhaps the most important thing you can do once you're given your word is ASK QUESTIONS, and I urge you to take full advantage of this. You can ask for all sorts of key information about the word you are given, which lets you confirm the correct spelling or at least make an educated guess.

A common mistake some spellers make is rushing to spell the word immediately after it's given—I strongly advise against this! To understand why, let's examine the word *stationery*. There is another word that is pronounced in exactly the same way but spelled differently: *stationary* (with an *a* instead of an *e*). Words like these, which are pronounced similarly or identically to others, are called homonyms. The difference between these two words is in the part of speech and definition: *stationery* with an *e* is a noun meaning "writing paper," whereas *stationary* with an *a* is an adjective meaning "staying

SPELLING ANYTHING

still." Asking for information like the part of speech and definition can clear up the confusion between these two words, whereas if you jumped right into spelling the word, you may end up spelling the wrong one and get eliminated. These are not the only types of information you can ask; in fact, you have a full 90 seconds to ask up to 8 different types of questions and then spell your word. It is key for you to utilize all the options that the spelling bee provides to try and spell your word correctly.

Akash's 7 Golden Questions

When I competed in the spelling bee, I made it a point to ask seven questions for every word I was asked. These questions were invaluable in helping me spell my words correctly. Here are the seven questions in order:

1. Are there any alternate pronunciations?
2. Am I pronouncing the word correctly?
3. Can I have the definition?
4. Can I have the language of origin?
5. Can I have the part of speech?
6. Can I have the word in a sentence?
7. Can you repeat the word again?

I strongly encourage you to ask these questions for EVERY word you're given, even if you immediately know how to spell it. Having this poster in your home or classroom is a great way to keep these seven rules in mind for the Spelling Bee. If you want to order one, just scan the QR code to access my Etsy shop. Asking these questions will greatly improve your chances of spelling words correctly, so let's go over these seven GOLDEN QUESTIONS to help solidify your spelling strategy.

SPELLING ANYTHING

A snapshot from my audition video for a TV show with Mr. Steve Harvey in 2015

Are There Any Alternate Pronunciations?

Asking for alternative pronunciations serves two key functions. First, it helps distinguish between homonyms and clarifies any confusing spellings. It is very common for spellers to confuse one word for another, especially if those words sound similar, and it's very important to ask for alternate pronunciations so that you can differentiate the words. For example, if you heard the word *accept*, it might sound exactly like the word *except*, which is pronounced /ik-'sept/. But if you asked for the alternate pronunciation, you would hear not just /ik-'sept/, but *also* the extra pronunciation /ak-'sept/.

This gives away that the only possible spelling would be *accept*.

Additionally, asking for alternate pronunciations could reveal important information you would have never known otherwise. If you were given the word *apoptosis*, for example, you might first hear the pronunciation /ˌa-pə-ˌtō-səs/, which may lead you to spell it "apo*t*osis." However, if you asked for the alternate pronunciation, you would immediately learn that there is another pronunciation, /ˌa-pəp-ˌtō-səs/, which indicates that there must be another *p* in the word: apo*p*tosis.

I always ask for alternate pronunciations as the first question because it can completely change how you look at the word. You might be able to disambiguate homonyms, spot roots easier, or even recall how to spell the word on the spot. So, always start by asking for alternate pronunciations!

Am I Pronouncing the Word Correctly?

The second question is to repeat the word back to the judges and ask if you're pronouncing the word correctly. This step ensures that the word you're thinking of is the same as the word the pronouncer has asked you. *Always* make sure to say the word out loud so the judges can confer and let you know whether you got it right. There are plenty of cases where spellers have misspelled words simply because they misheard the pronouncer, and asking this question can avoid that from happening.

As an example, the first word that I was ever asked onstage at a spelling bee was the word "brush." I was 2 years old back then, and I misheard the pronouncer as saying the word "burst" instead of "brush," so, I spelled B-U-R-S-T! That's why it's important to make sure that the word you're given and the word you're thinking of are the same by asking whether you are pronouncing the word correctly.

Some spelling bees might not directly answer the question "Am I pronouncing the word correctly?", and that's usually because the judges will automatically correct you if they notice a mistake in your pronunciation. Even still, I always make a point to ask this question, as a way of reminding the judges to listen to whether

I'm pronouncing the word correctly or not. Ultimately, it's essential to ensure the judges correct you if you mispronounce a word, as failing to do so could lead to a misspelling and elimination from the bee. Be careful about pronouncing your word correctly, as accurate pronunciation is the most critical factor in determining whether you spell it right or not.

Can I Have the Definition?

The definition is usually the best hint you can get to spell the word correctly. Asking for the definition can differentiate between homonyms, pinpoint certain roots in the word, and connect the word to other words that you might already know. Homonyms are a common pitfall for many spellers, and asking the definition is a simple way to overcome them. The *stationery/stationary* example from earlier is one example of how important the definition is.

It is much easier to pinpoint certain roots in the word you are asked when you know the definition. As an example, if you asked for the definition of the word *chlorophyll*, you would hear "a green pigment found in leaves." This immediately confirms that the word contains the Greek roots *chloro-* (green) and *-phyll* (leaf), resulting in the complete spelling, *chlorophyll*.

Connecting the word you are asked to other words you already know is another crucial skill that the definition allows you to use. If you heard the word *asteroidal* and were trying to connect it to another word, you can ask for the definition: "relating to a type of celestial body." From there, you would be able to connect the word with *asteroid* and spell it correctly.

Out of all the 7 Golden Questions, "Can I have the definition?" is by far the most informative question you can ask, because it provides a wealth of information you can use to spell your word correctly. This is a question you simply cannot afford to skip!

Can I Have the Language of Origin?

The language of origin helps identify the word's spelling patterns, roots, and rules specific to that language, providing valuable clues for spelling the word correctly. For example, if the word was *mousse* \müs\ and you asked for the language of origin, you would hear that the word is French. From there, just apply the French spelling rules from Chapter 5 and you can easily figure out the spelling of each sound in the word: the \m\ sound is spelled *m*, the \ü\ is spelled *ou*, and the \s\ sound at the end is usually *-sse*. Using only the language of origin and your understanding of spelling rules, you can spell the word *mousse*. While it may feel complicated to piece this together initially, as you become more familiar with the spelling patterns of different languages, you'll find yourself spelling words from these languages with increasing ease. By asking for the language of origin, you can gain greater insights into the spelling of this word.

5

Can I Have the Part of Speech?

The part of speech can help you determine word endings and differentiate between homonym pairs.

The suffixes used in many words change depending on the part of speech. Adjectives usually end in *-ous*, adverbs tend to end in *-ly*, and verbs can end in *-ing* or *-ed*. As explained in Chapter 5, nouns ending in *-us* or *-um* tend to come from Latin, which can help you reinforce those spellings in words like *animus* and *minimum*. Asking for the part of speech can help resolve confusing word endings. For example, if you ask for the part of speech of the word *octopus*, you'll learn it's a noun, indicating it should end in *-us* (a noun ending) rather than *-ous* (an adjective ending).

Additionally, the part of speech can clarify homonyms and other tricky word pairs. For instance, *affect* is a verb, while *effect* is a noun; similarly, *advise* is a verb, and *advice* is a noun. In the spelling bee, a competition where every detail counts, asking for the part of speech can easily improve accuracy.

Can I Have the Word in a Sentence?

Asking for the word in a sentence helps you picture the word in context, making it easier to spell. A sentence can instantly resolve the ambiguity of homonyms. For example, consider the homophones *capital* and *capitol*. If you ask for the word in a sentence, you might hear: "Washington, D.C. is the *capital* of the United States," which points to the city where the government is centered (*capital*). Alternatively, "The legislators met at the state *capitol* to pass the new bill" clearly indicates *capitol*, the building where government sessions occur. Although the information in the sentence may overlap with what you learn from the definition or part of speech, it can still offer valuable context to refresh your memory. I strongly encourage you to ask for the sentence, as it can make all the difference in spelling tricky words correctly.

Can You Repeat the Word?

The final question, "Can you repeat the word?", is the most important one because it ensures you have correctly remembered the word you've been asked to spell. Even if you're confident, there are times when you might mishear or miss a subtle detail—such as confusing *reassured* with *reassure* (omitting the D at the end). In a competition where precision is everything, you must be absolutely certain that the word you are about to spell is exactly the same as what the pronouncer has given you. This is why it's essential to always ask the pronouncer to repeat the word.

Say It - Spell It - Say It

When spelling a word, always use the pattern: **Say It - Spell It - Say It**. For example, if your word is *apple*, you would say: "Apple - A-P-P-L-E - Apple." This method is crucial because it clearly signals to the judges when you start spelling and finish spelling. While this is not an official rule at the National Spelling Bee, it is strongly encouraged. In practice bees, however, this format might be strictly enforced, so it's a good habit to adopt.

It's essential to practice the 7 Golden Questions and the Say It - Spell It - Say It technique regularly. When a family member or friend quizzes you, make it a habit to ask these questions to simulate the experience of a real spelling bee. This practice will not only help you develop the habit of asking these questions consistently but also deepen your understanding of how to effectively use the information they provide.

Asking for Roots

There is also an eighth type of question, asking about roots. If you think that the word you are given may contain a specific root, ask the judges to confirm. There will usually be a judge who checks the dictionary for any roots, and if you can provide a) a root, b) its language of origin, and c) its meaning, the judges will give you an answer about whether you got the root right. The judges need *all three* of those parts to be correct for them to say that you're on the right track. For example, if you heard the word *aureous*, you could ask "Does this derive from the Latin root *aur-* meaning 'gold'?" and the pronouncer would respond either "Yes" or "You're on the right track," which usually means you got it right. However, if you asked "Does this derive from the Latin root *or-* meaning 'mouth'?", the pronouncer would respond, "I don't see that here," meaning you got the root wrong or provided the wrong information. This is a more expert-level question, so if you aren't completely familiar with roots yet, then you can skip this question for now.

Lastly, keep in mind that you have just 90 seconds to ask your questions and spell the word. The QR code is an example of me asking all 7 of these questions at the National Spelling Bee (back when the time limit was 2 minutes long). If remembering all the questions feels overwhelming, you might consider asking, "Can I have all of the information?" as a shortcut. However, especially in smaller regional bees, the pronouncer may accidentally skip key details. For this reason, it's best to stick to the 7 Golden Rules to ensure you don't miss anything important!

What to Do If You Don't Know Your Word

Nearly every speller has been in a situation where they don't know the word they've been given. The *Merriam-Webster Unabridged* dictionary has over half a million words, so it is rather likely that a speller gets a word they are not familiar with. It's important for you to know how you can deal with this, so let's go over some strategies to use onstage if you aren't sure about the spelling of your word.

Don't Panic

Perhaps the biggest tip is not to panic! As mentioned above, feeling nervous is completely normal, but if you can stay calm and composed, you will be able to suppress the instinct of panicking and focus on the word at hand. The key is to just stay calm, ask the 7 Golden Questions, and utilize all the information given to you. After all, you have studied very hard to get to this point, and now is the time for you to channel all of your knowledge into spelling the word correctly. Even if you're unsure, giving your best attempt is always better than panicking and freezing up. Keep in mind that this is part of what makes the spelling bee such a challenge. Stay composed, think through your word, and give it your best shot!

Use Language Rules and Roots

The language rules and roots you learned in Chapters 5 and 6 are by far your most important tool if you don't know a word. Approach words based on language, and think about not only the rules themselves, but whether there is a possibility for exceptions. Take the French word *cachepot* \\'kash-₁pät, 'kash-₁pō, 'ka-shə-₁pō\\, a type of container that holds a flower pot. The first part of the word can be pronounced \\'kash\\ or \\'ka-shə\\ – the \\k\\ is spelled *c* and the \\a\\ is spelled *a*, but because the \\sh\\ sound, which is spelled *ch*, is usually followed by a vowel letter, there has to be an *e* right after it. This makes the most likely spelling of the first part *cache-*. The ending of this word can be pronounced \-pō\, which has many different spellings because of the \ō\ sound, but crucially, it can also be pronounced \-pät\. There's only one ending with both of those pronunciations, *-pot*, and when combined with the meaning (container holding a flower *pot*), it becomes clear that the ending is *-pot*. Combining these two parts gives us *cachepot*. This process gives you a step-by-step guide to spelling a difficult word using just the information given to you, the spelling rules of the root language, and your intuition. In reality, most words are not going to be this hard to figure out, but this shows that if you can think through the different parts of a word, you will be able to take care of even the more challenging words easily.

Use Your Knowledge of Related Words

Using your knowledge of related words is another crucial technique to use when you encounter an unfamiliar word because it helps you make educated guesses based on patterns, roots, and meanings. Words often share common roots, prefixes, or suffixes with other words you may already know, giving you clues about their structure and spelling. For instance, I spelled the word *gneissoid* correctly at a practice bee; it means "relating to a specific type of rock". I recollected the existing word *gneiss*, which refers to the same thing. Recognizing these connections allows you to break down unknown words into familiar components, increasing your chances of spelling them correctly. This strategy is especially useful for words that are complex or come from languages with many spelling rules, because even an educated guess may not be enough to spell the word right.

Don't Overcomplicate

Many words follow straightforward spelling rules, and second-guessing yourself by adding extra letters or using uncommon spelling patterns can steer you in the wrong direction. Instead of assuming every word is exceptionally difficult, trust the basics of what you've learned—language patterns and roots. Overcomplicating words wastes valuable time and energy, so focus on clear, logical thinking. If you have absolutely no idea how to spell the word you're given, just KEEP IT SIMPLE.

These techniques are the best ways of spelling words you don't know when you're on stage. Of course, there is an element of luck to it, but the more you learn, the more it becomes a game of skill.

CHAPTER 9

After the Bee

THE EXCITEMENT AND INTENSITY OF the spelling bee may have ended, but what comes next is just as important as the competition itself. Whether you walked away with the trophy or faced the dreaded bell, this moment offers an opportunity to grow and prepare for what lies ahead. Winning your local bee means stepping up to the challenge of higher-level bees, bringing new words, tougher competition, and greater stakes. On the other hand, losing doesn't mean the end—it's a chance to learn from the experience and come back even stronger. In this chapter, we'll explore what to do after the bee, whether you're gearing up for the next competition or reflecting on how to improve for the future.

What Happens If You Win?

Your hard work paid off! You've worked for many days, weeks, months, and maybe even years to get to this point, and now you're moving up to the next level of competition. If you have advanced to your next regional level, your victory should be a great boost of confidence and encouragement. It shows that you're going in the right path, and if you work a little bit more and win your next bee, you will become one step closer to winning your golden ticket to the National Spelling Bee.

If you became the champion at your regional bee, CONGRATULATIONS, you have won an all-expenses-paid trip to Washington, D.C., to represent your area at the Scripps National Spelling Bee! You are

Nine-year-old me after winning the 2019 San Angelo Regional Spelling Bee

Standing outside the Maryland Ballroom at the Gaylord National Resort & Convention Center in National Harbor, Oxon Hill, Maryland, the iconic venue for the Scripps National Spelling Bee

now in the elite group of the best spellers in the nation, an incredible achievement that you should pat yourself on the back for. Your regional spelling bee officials will give you all the details about how to register for the Scripps National Spelling Bee (as I explained in Chapter 3). Below are some of the prizes and perks that come by winning your regional bee:

1. Regional/state spelling bee championship trophy
2. All-expenses-paid trip to Washington, D.C.
3. *Merriam-Webster's Unabridged* 1-year online subscription
4. *Encyclopedia Britannica* online subscription
5. Jay Sugarman Award (U.S. Mint proof set)

6. Maybe even prize money from your regional bee

As you are representing your region at the national level, local media will likely want to highlight your success. While the attention can be exciting, it might also feel overwhelming if you're not sure how to handle it. The following tips can help you feel confident in front of the cameras.

Be Prepared

Reporters tend to ask regional champions about their preparation, favorite words, or how they feel about advancing to the Nationals. Take a moment to think about what you'd like to share. If you get an interview opportunity after the bee, practice answering common questions with a family member or friend to feel more comfortable.

Stay Humble

Whether you're being interviewed on camera or quoted in a newspaper, express gratitude to those who supported you—your parents, teachers, or coaches. Acknowledging others shows humility and makes a great impression.

Be Professional

While it's important to relax and be yourself, remember that this is an opportunity to represent your community. Dress appropriately for interviews and speak clearly to leave a positive impression.

News coverage is a way to celebrate your hard work and inspire others through your achievements. Embrace the spotlight with pride, and use it as motivation to keep working even harder for the National Spelling Bee!

What Happens If You Misspell?

Appealing Your Elimination

If you misspell your word and believe you were given incorrect information, you can appeal your elimination with the bee staff. Only pursue an appeal if you're confident that part of the information provided was incorrect—always double-check the word you missed in *Merriam-Webster Unabridged* to verify. If you decide to proceed, approach a staff member (usually not the judging panel) and state that you wish to appeal your elimination. Follow their instructions, which may involve making an oral request or filling out a form to submit for consideration. Be sure to clearly explain why you believe your elimination was unfair, and most importantly, submit your appeal BEFORE THE END OF THE ROUND! Many bees will NOT accept appeals submitted after the round is over, even if your claim is correct. At Nationals, spellers cannot appeal if they received the correct pronunciation and definition, regardless of any other information. The appeal system can vary depending on your regional bees, so it's a good idea to ask your local bee organizers about their specific rules ahead of time.

After the round ends, the judges will review your appeal and decide whether to accept or reject it. If the appeal is accepted, you may be given a new word to spell to determine if you will advance to the next round. If it is rejected, your original elimination remains in effect. Keep in mind that the judges' decisions are final, and it's important to respect the outcome of the appeal process.

If You Get Eliminated

Handling success is easy; facing adversity is much more challenging. No speller wins every bee they compete in, and that's OK. By following the tips in this book, there's a fair chance that you could have placed first and become your regional champion, or at least made it to the top three. But even if you didn't, what truly matters isn't just your final placement—it's the time, effort, and dedication you put into preparing for the competition. Knowing that you gave it your all is an achievement in itself. No matter what place you got, you should feel very proud of yourself because you didn't give up – you prepared very hard, showed up at the competition, and presented yourself on the stage before the mic. YOU ARE A WINNER!

SPELLING ANYTHING

Eight-year-old me after becoming the runner-up at the 2018 San Angelo Regional Spelling Bee

If you're in seventh grade or below, you still have at least one more year of eligibility in the Scripps National Spelling Bee, so if you hear the dreaded bell sound, don't get disappointed or give up. Treat yourself by taking a day or two to rest and do what you enjoy doing because you put in the hard work and came very far. Then, start working hard for next year because if you plan right, you'll be the CHAMPION next year!

11-year-old me after winning the 2021 San Angelo Regional Spelling Bee

Most people tend to remember their losses for the first few days, the first week, maybe the first month. However, the person who remembers until next year's bee and has the burning desire to avenge their loss will eventually emerge as the next champion. The losses that sting the most are often the ones that fuel future success, so channel that energy into your preparation. Reflect on your performance at your local bee(s) to identify what led you to miss your word. Was it a tricky root, an unfamiliar language pattern, a confusing exception, a missed detail in the word information, or perhaps something else entirely? Use this as an opportunity to refine your study strategies and set new goals for the year ahead. For example, if you learned that you struggle with words of unknown origin, you can spend some time getting used to those words so that they don't spell trouble for you when you're on stage.

Once you know what you need to focus on, formulate a plan on how you will achieve your goal over the coming year. Start with a long-term plan, and then break it down into short-term goals aimed at specific topics or fields. Ask yourself: What were my weak areas? How can I strengthen them? And most importantly, how can I stay motivated for next year? Implement the answers to these questions into your study schedule. With dedication, consistency, and a solid plan, you'll return stronger and ready to claim the championship next year!

12-year-old me and my family after I won the 2022 San Angelo Regional Spelling Bee

If you are in eighth grade, then I'm sorry to say that this is where your Scripps National Spelling Bee journey ends. However, it doesn't have to be the end of your spelling adventure. If you're passionate about continuing, there are high school competitions to explore. For example, Texas hosts UIL, a statewide league that includes a spelling competition alongside academic, athletic, and performative events. If your state or region has something similar, it's a fantastic way to keep pursuing your love for the English language. Additionally, with all the experience you have gained, sharing your knowledge and strategies can make a real difference while keeping you connected to the spelling bee world. You can use your spelling knowledge to support others, like your younger siblings, cousins, or friends who are planning on competing at the spelling bee. Just remember one thing: You may not have won the spelling bee, but you haven't truly lost anything. In fact, you've acquired a rich vocabulary base, a wealth of knowledge, and skills that will serve you well in any career path you choose. The hours you spent preparing, learning, and pushing yourself have already made you stronger and smarter. The benefits of this spelling journey will stay with you forever, shaping your future in ways you couldn't imagine. You've achieved something remarkable—that's worth celebrating because your life journey has only just begun!

SPELLING ANYTHING

(Left) 13-year-old me after winning my final San Angelo Regional Spelling Bee in 2023

(Bottom) 13-year-old me, competing at my final Scripps National Spelling Bee in 2023

Get in Touch with Akash

@AkashVukoti

AkashVukoti.com

You can email me at:
Akash@AkashVukoti.com

www.ingramcontent.com/pod-product-compliance
Lightning Source LLC
Jackson TN
JSHW011909150425
82668JS00016B/771